ROAD BIKE

North
Georgia

25 GREAT RIDES IN THE
MOUNTAINS AND VALLEYS
OF NORTH GEORGIA

Jim Parham

milestone
press

almond, nc

Book design by Ron Roman
Cover photo by Mary Ellen Hammond

Milestone Press, P.O. Box 158, Almond, NC 28702
www.milestonepress.com

Library of Congress Cataloging-In-Publication Data

Parham, Jim.
  Road bike north Georgia : 25 great rides in the mountains
  and valleys of North Georgia / Jim Parham.
       p.   cm.
  ISBN 1-889596-04-3
  1. Bicycle touring—Georgia—Guidebooks. 2. Georgia—
Guidebooks. I. Title.
  GV1045.5.G28P37 1998
  796.6'3'09758—dc21   98-10276
                                                    CIP

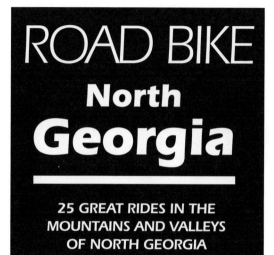

ROAD BIKE

North
Georgia

25 GREAT RIDES IN THE
MOUNTAINS AND VALLEYS
OF NORTH GEORGIA

Jim Parham

Contents

Geographical Areas

Introduction

There is no better way to see and experience the roadways of North Georgia than from a bicycle. This top portion of the state is a geologic mixture of flat-topped plateaus, mountain ridges and green valleys. At the same time it is a cultural mix of isolated wilderness, mountain farm communities and small towns. Through these areas you'll find paved roads spreading out in all directions, and many of them make for a great place to ride your road bike.

This guidebook outlines 25 of the best road bike rides in North Georgia, and is written for the cyclist who enjoys morning, afternoon or all-day bike rides. All the routes follow paved roads, and although almost any kind of bike will do, they will be more enjoyable on a road bike equipped with gearing suitable for mountainous terrain. Whether you're a first-time cyclist, a hard core roadie or something in between, you'll find a lot of options.

Lookout Mountain slices through the northwestern corner of the state as it drops down out of Chattanooga, Tennessee. This plateau and the Chickamauga Valley that spreads out below it are home to some of the most scenic rides in the state. This area is rich in the history of the American Civil War, too. Several routes begin at Chickamauga National Battlefield Park. To the south, just above Rome, is Berry College and the Armuchee Ridges. Here you can ride for miles through the beautiful 30,000-acre Berry campus, or venture out through the quiet, rolling farmland to the north.

Farther to the east, you'll encounter North Georgia's rugged Blue Ridge Mountains. In this part of the state it's easy to begin many rides right from the courthouse squares of little mountain towns. Parking and leaving your vehicle is not a problem and you can be out into the countryside before you break a sweat. Here rides are based out of Ellijay, Dahlonega, Helen and Clayton. Ellijay is the heart of Georgia's apple growing region. Expect to ride through orchards in some stage of production most any time of year. Dahlonega and Helen butt up against the highest mountains in the state. If you head very far north out of either of these towns, count on some really big climbs. The mountainous region around Clayton is known for its lakes. Rides here traverse the edges of these lakes and climb into the surrounding hills.

Nowhere in North Georgia is the terrain truly flat. Even a ride a local would describe as level and easy might seem quite hilly to someone who has never ridden in the mountains. That said, the routes in this book are broken up into easy, easy/moderate,

moderate and difficult rides. With each ride description I've given an estimated time allowance based on ability level, directions to the start of each route, basic characteristics of the ride and any special hazards to look out for. Directly following this information you'll find a route map and an elevation profile. Look to the back of the book for turn-by-turn directions. In choosing a ride it is most important to look at the total distance, the estimated time allowance and the elevation profile. With this information alone, you should be able to tell pretty quick if this is a ride you are up for and can enjoy. The brief description of each route is intended to give you just enough information to whet your appetite—you can discover the rest for yourself. This book is small for a reason. Tuck it in a baggie and take it with you.

North Georgia's mild climate affords year-round riding enjoyment. Granted, there can be quite a few days in the winter months when it is just too cold, wet and nasty out to ride on the roads. However, just as many days *are* suitable for cycling, especially for the diehard. In spring, summer and fall, the weather is ideal. You can look forward to cool-to-warm days in both spring and fall, with the coolest temperatures occurring at the higher elevations. Spring brings a succession of wildflowers, and autumn here is famous for bright, colorful foliage. Summer in Georgia is downright hot and the humidity can make the air seem as thick as goo. You'll find the mountains to be the best place to ride at this time of the year. There's nothing like a good six-mile downhill to cool you off.

Regardless of the season, make sure you go prepared. Many of the routes are within reasonable driving distance of a bike shop. There's a shop listing on page 9 so you can find the one closest to where you plan to ride. Once you're on the road, though, you are on your own. At best you'll pass by small country stores and gas stations. Some routes are so remote you won't pass any sort of store at all. Take plenty to drink and eat, adequate clothing for the time of year, a pump and spare tube, and a good assortment of tools that you know how to use.

Road biking in North Georgia is fantastic. If you do only a few of these rides or every single one, as I have, the experience will become a memory you won't forget. I hope you enjoy the use of this book time and time again.

J.P.
April 1998

he bicycle is legally considered a vehicle in Georgia. Thus bicyclists have full rights and responsibilities on the roadway and are subject to the regulations governing the operation of a motor vehicle, where applicable.

Georgia traffic laws require the rider of a bicycle to:
- Obey all signs, signals, and pavement markings.
- Signal all turns and stops using the standard hand signals.
- Ride in the same direction as traffic, never facing oncoming vehicles.
- Ride no more than two abreast.
- Use a bicycle path near the roadway, if one is provided.
- Avoid interstate or controlled access highways.
- Keep at least one hand on the handlebars at all times.
- Avoid hanging on to moving vehicles by any method.
- Use an attached seat when carrying a passenger.
- Use a bicycle with brakes strong enough to skid the wheels on dry pavement.

In addition:
- Every bicycle in use at nighttime must have a headlight visible from at least 300 feet ahead and a red rear reflector visible from 300 feet to the rear.
- It is unlawful to alter a bicycle so as to cause the pedal in its lowest position to be more than 12 inches above the ground.
- No child between the ages of one year and four years shall ride as a passenger on a bicycle unless securely seated in a child passenger seat or bicycle trailer and wearing a helmet.
- No person under the age of 16 years shall operate a bicycle unless wearing a bicycle helmet.

To insure a safe trip:
- Always wear a bicycle helmet
- Carry plenty of liquids
- Avoid biking at night
- When riding with a group, ride single file
- Wear bright clothing to increase visibility
- Be sure your bicycle is the right size for you and in good repair

Remember, the bicyclist always loses in a conflict with a motor vehicle. Ride defensively and in a predictable manner to avoid accidents. Be courteous to other drivers. Keep traffic flowing by helping motorists pass you in a safe manner.

North GA Bike Shops

Rome

Bob's Bicycle Shop
2203 Shorter Ave.
Rome, GA 30161
706-291-1501

Pullen's Ordinary Bicycles
105 Broad Street
Rome, GA 30161
706-234-2453

Dalton

Dalton Bicycle Works
1107 E. Dalton Ave.
Dalton, GA 30721
706-279-2558

Ellijay

Cartecay Bike Shop
52 North Main St
Ellijay, GA 30540
706-635-BIKE

Dahlonega

Mountain Adventures Cyclery
52 Clayton Drive
Dahlonega, GA 30533
706-864-8525

Chattanooga

East Ridge Bikes
5910 Ringold Rd.
Chattanooga, TN 37412
423-894-9122

River City Bicycles
112 Tremont St.
Chattanooga, TN 37405
423-265-7176

The Bike Shop
201 Frazier Ave.
Chattanooga, TN 37505
423-267-1000

Blue Ridge

Cycle South
4295A Old Hwy 76
Blue Ridge, GA 30513
706-632-3533

Helen

Woody's Mountain Bikes
Hwy. 356
Helen, GA 30545
706-878-3715

Gainesville

Biketown USA
1604 Dawsonville Hwy.
Gainesville, GA 30501
770-532-7090

The area locator map above serves as a general reference for all the starting points in this book. Start locations are marked with a star ★. For turn-by-turn directions and a detailed map for a specific ride, refer to the individual route description.

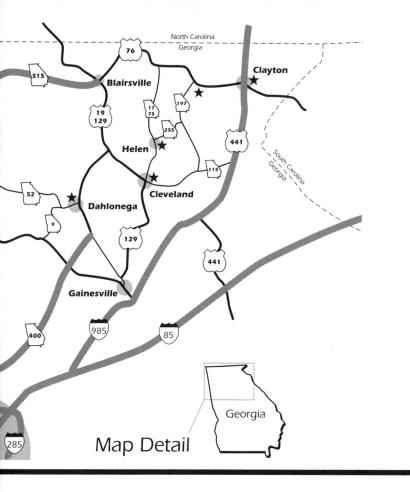

Map Detail

Chickamauga Battlefield

Rating: Easy   **9 Miles**

This ride is rated easy because of its length and the flat terrain.

A very pleasant ride as well as a trip through history—be sure to take time to read the historical markers and look at the monuments. This route passes through quiet woods and traverses open battle fields. The scenery is very pretty and there's a good chance of seeing wildlife, especially deer. It's a popular area for hikers, bikers and tourists, as well.

Estimated Riding Times
- Beginner: 1 - 1.5 hours
- Intermediate: 45 minutes - 1 hour
- Advanced: 30 - 45 minutes

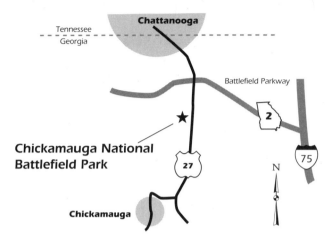

Directions to the Start
- Ride begins at Battlefield Visitor Center at north end of Park off US 27, north of the town of Chickamauga

Alternate Start: Any of the picnic areas along the route

Ride Characteristics & Cautions
- Most of the route follows quiet, narrow, 1-way battlefield touring roads
- There are 2 short stretches following US 27 which can have very busy traffic

Points of Interest
- Many, many battlefield monuments and historical markers

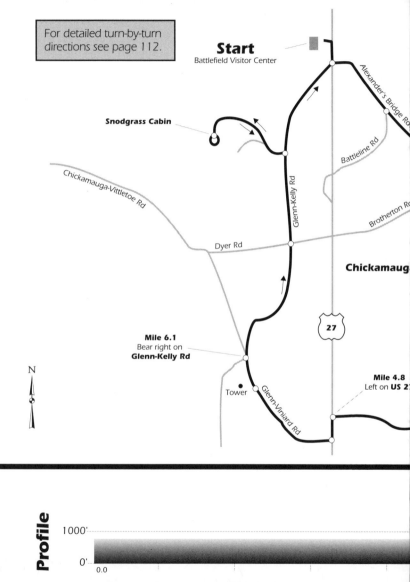

For detailed turn-by-turn directions see page 112.

Start
Battlefield Visitor Center

Snodgrass Cabin

Alexander's Bridge Rd

Battleline Rd

Chickamauga-Vittletoe Rd

Glenn-Kelly Rd

Brotherton Rd

Dyer Rd

Chickamaug

27

Mile 6.1
Bear right on
Glenn-Kelly Rd

N

Tower

Glenn-Viniard Rd

Mile 4.8
Left on **US 2**

Profile

1000'

0'
0.0

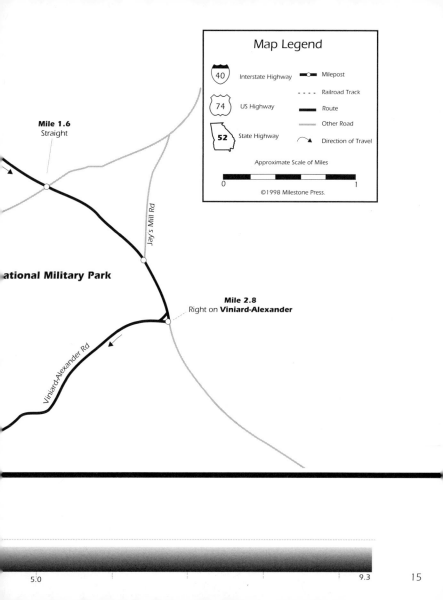

Map Legend

40 Interstate Highway		●▬● Milepost
74 US Highway		- - - - Railroad Track
52 State Highway		▬▬▬ Route
		Other Road
		↷ Direction of Travel

Approximate Scale of Miles

0 _____ 1

©1998 Milestone Press.

Mile 1.6
Straight

Jay's Mill Rd

ational Military Park

Mile 2.8
Right on **Viniard-Alexander**

Viniard-Alexander Rd

5.0   9.3

Berry College

Rating: Easy   11 Miles

This ride is rated easy because of its short length and because it is very flat.

Berry College has the largest campus of any college in the world—close to 30,000 acres. Even with two campuses, there are plenty of wide open spaces left over. This ride takes you from the college campus out and around the mountain campus and back. Both campuses are beautiful with dramatic stone buildings, log cabins, classic dairy barns and manicured gardens. The whole area is a wildlife refuge, so you can expect to see an abundance of deer and birds, and maybe even a fox or two.

Estimated Riding Times
- Beginner: 1.5 - 2 hours
- Intermediate: 1 - 1.5 hour
- Advanced: 45 minutes - 1 hour

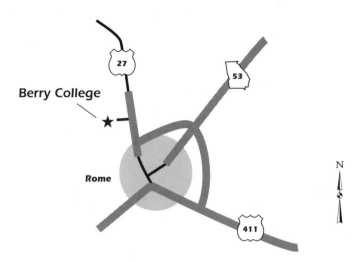

Directions to the Start
- Park in the visitor parking lot, behind either Krannert Center or Hermann Hall.
- Start the ride from the flagpole roundabout in front of Hermann Hall

Ride Characteristics & Cautions
- Ride is on quiet campus roads and designated bike path
- On the main campus, watch for students in the crosswalks

Points of Interest
- Ford Buildings
- Frost Chapel
- Swan Lake
- Old Dairy Barns and many different breeds of cattle
- Martha Berry Museum (just across US 27)

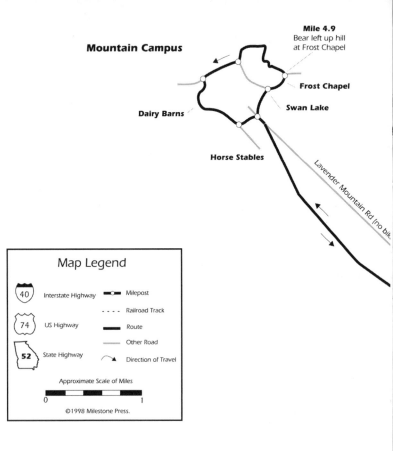

Mountain Campus

Mile 4.9
Bear left up hill
at Frost Chapel

Frost Chapel

Swan Lake

Dairy Barns

Horse Stables

Lavender Mountain Rd (no bik...

Map Legend

(40) Interstate Highway

(74) US Highway

(52) State Highway

Milepost

Railroad Track

Route

Other Road

Direction of Travel

Approximate Scale of Miles

0   1

©1998 Milestone Press.

Profile

1000'

0'

Ford Buildings

Mountain Campu...

0.0   5.0

For detailed turn-by-turn directions see page 113.

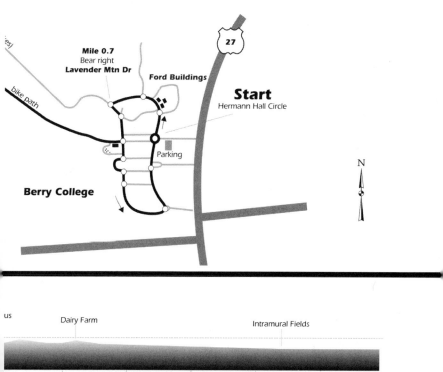

Mile 0.7
Bear right
Lavender Mtn Dr

Ford Buildings

27

Start
Hermann Hall Circle

bike path

Parking

Berry College

N

us

Dairy Farm

Intramural Fields

10.8

19

Corbin Hill

Rating: Easy   9 Miles

This is a short and easy ride, especially if you start from town, but it does include a few hills that will get your attention.

 This ride starts with a short but steep climb up Corbin Hill. Take your time and absorb the beautiful view overlooking downtown Ellijay. Once up top, you'll ride through a big apple orchard, and depending on the season you'll see pink blossoms, green apples or bright red fruit ready for harvest. From here, the rural, rolling countryside is dotted with interesting barns here and there, all along very quiet roads. Since you gain most of your elevation at the beginning of the ride, the rest is spent gradually working your way back down to town.

Estimated Riding Times
- Beginner: 1.5 - 2 hours
- Intermediate: 1 hour
- Advanced: 45 minutes - 1 hour

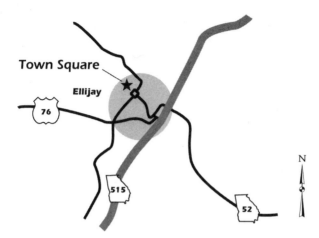

Directions to the Start
- Ride starts at the town square in the heart of Ellijay

Ride Characteristics & Cautions
- The first half-mile is pretty steep
- Watch for loose dogs in the roadway
- There are 2 steep downhills that lead right into a stop sign and a right turn at mileposts 5.2 and 7.3
- Some of the roadways are a bit on the bumpy side

Points of Interest
- Corbin Hill view
- Apple Orchard

Corbin Hill

For detailed turn-by-turn
directions see page 114.

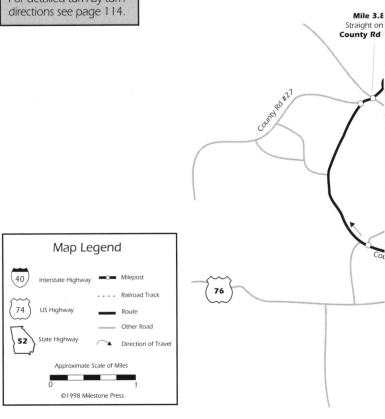

Mile 3.8
Straight on
County Rd

County Rd #27

Map Legend

(40) Interstate Highway   ●━● Milepost

(74) US Highway   - - - - Railroad Track

━━━ Route

(52) State Highway   ──── Other Road

➤ Direction of Travel

Approximate Scale of Miles

0   1

©1998 Milestone Press.

(76)

Profile

Corbin Hill

Cross GA 5

2000'

1000'

0.0

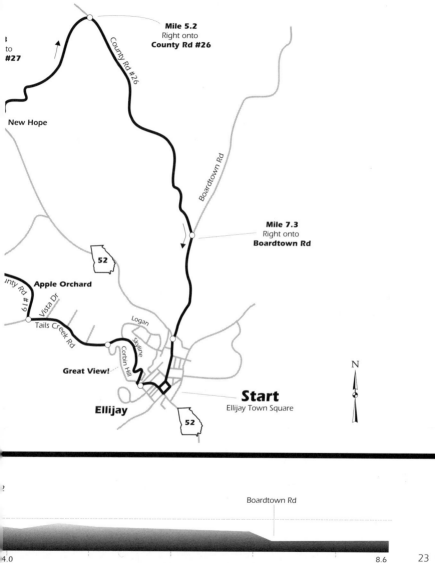

Mile 5.2
Right onto
County Rd #26

to
#27

County Rd #26

New Hope

Boardtown Rd

Mile 7.3
Right onto
Boardtown Rd

52

Apple Orchard

County Rd #19

Vista Dr

Tails Creek Rd

Logan

Skyline

Corbin Hill

Great View!

Ellijay

52

Start
Ellijay Town Square

N

Boardtown Rd

4.0   8.6

Old 5 Roundtop

Rating: Easy   22 Miles

This ride is rated easy since most of it is on relatively flat terrain. You can expect one short but fairly steep climb up to Roundtop.

Old Georgia Highway 5 parallels the new four-lane Highway GA 515 for a number of miles south of Ellijay. This is a perfect example of how a new road can suck the life out of an older one. Riding along, you'll notice boarded up and falling down businesses and kudzu creeping further and further onto the road. This is great for cyclists, though, because there's very little traffic. Leaving Old 5 you'll climb to the little community of Roundtop and then descend through pretty farm valleys along secluded roadways before returning on Old 5 itself.

Estimated Riding Times
- Beginner: 2.5 - 3 hours
- Intermediate: 2 hours
- Advanced: 1.5 hours

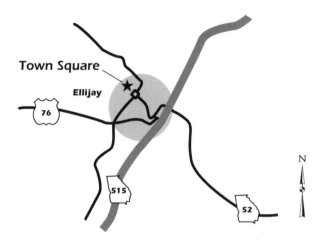

Directions to the Start
- Ride starts at the town square in the heart of Ellijay

Ride Characteristics & Cautions
- Traffic can be a little tricky close to town
- Knight Road is fairly bumpy
- Watch for loose dogs
- Check your speed on GA 382 at mile 18. It's a fast downhill stop followed by a left turn onto Old 5

Points of Interest
- Coosawatee River
- Downtown Ellijay
- Battered old store fronts on Old 5

For detailed turn-by-turn
directions see page 114.

COOSAWATEE RIV

Map Legend

(40) Interstate Highway

(74) US Highway

(52) State Highway

━●━ Milepost

- - - - Railroad Track

━━━ Route

──── Other Road

↷▲ Direction of Travel

Approximate Scale of Miles

1   0   1

©1998 Milestone Press.

Mile 12.6
Left on **Knight Rd**

Mile 10
Right on **Round**

Profile

2000'

Old 5

1000'

0.0

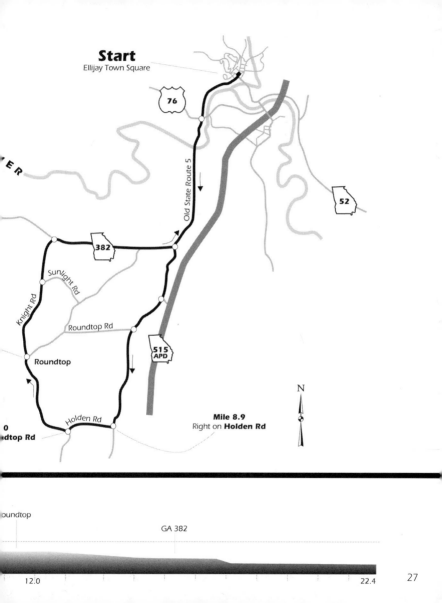

Start
Ellijay Town Square

76

Old State Route 5

382

52

Sunlight Rd

Knight Rd

Roundtop Rd

Roundtop

515
APD

Holden Rd

0
dtop Rd

Mile 8.9
Right on **Holden Rd**

N

oundtop

GA 382

12.0   22.4

Chickamauga Valley

Rating: Easy/Moderate   17 Miles

This ride is rated easy to moderate. Its terrain and length make it easy. The traffic on Mission Ridge Road ups the difficulty just a bit.

During the American Civil War the entire Chickamauga Valley was a buzz of activity as troops moved between Chattanooga, Lookout Mountain and Chickamauga. This ride follows quiet roads as it leaves the beautiful Chickamauga Battlefield Park and passes through the town of Chickamauga with its lovely historic homes. The route continues into rolling countryside with views of Lookout Mountain and Missionary Ridge before returning to the broad sweeping fields of the Battlefield Park.

Estimated Riding Times
- Beginner: 3 hours
- Intermediate: 2 hours
- Advanced: 1.5 hours

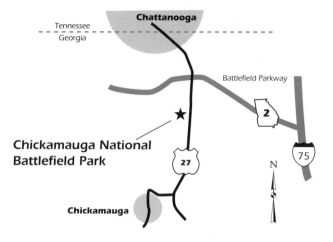

Chattanooga

Tennessee
- -
Georgia

Battlefield Parkway

★

Chickamauga National Battlefield Park

27

N

2

75

Chickamauga

Directions to the Start
- Ride begins at Battlefield Visitor Center at north end of Park off US 27, north of the town of Chickamauga

Ride Characteristics & Cautions
- With the exception of Mission Ridge Road, most of route follows quiet country backroads
- The northern section of Mission Ridge Road can be busy, especially in early morning and late afternoon
- This is a great Sunday morning ride

Points of Interest
- Chickamauga National Battlefield Park
- Older homes in the town of Chickamauga

Chickamauga Valley

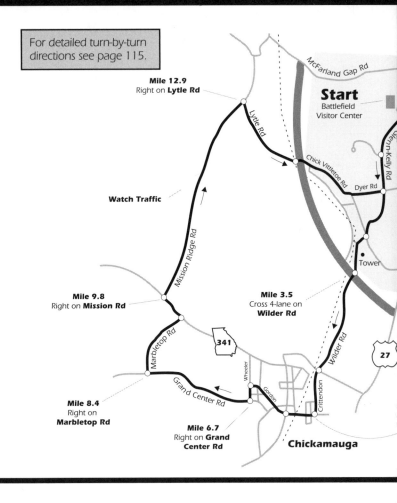

For detailed turn-by-turn directions see page 115.

Mile 12.9
Right on **Lytle Rd**

Lytle Rd

Start
Battlefield
Visitor Center

McFarland Gap Rd

Chick Vittletoe Rd

Dyer Rd

Glenn-Kelly Rd

Watch Traffic

Mission Ridge Rd

Tower

Mile 9.8
Right on **Mission Rd**

Mile 3.5
Cross 4-lane on
Wilder Rd

Marbletop Rd

341

Wheeler

Gordon

Grand Center Rd

Wilder Rd

Crittendon

27

Mile 8.4
Right on
Marbletop Rd

Mile 6.7
Right on **Grand
Center Rd**

Chickamauga

Profile

Town of Chickamauga

1000'

0'   0.0

30

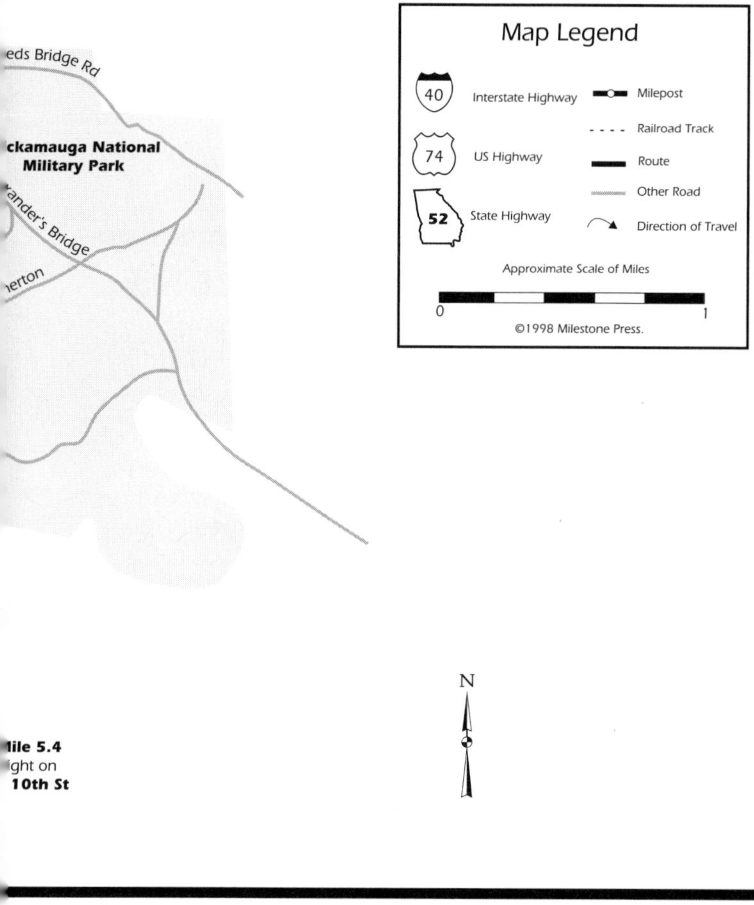

eds Bridge Rd

**ckamauga National
Military Park**

ander's Bridge

erton

Map Legend

40	Interstate Highway	●━●	Milepost
74	US Highway	- - - -	Railroad Track
52	State Highway	▬▬▬	Route
		~~	Other Road
			Direction of Travel

Approximate Scale of Miles

0   1

©1998 Milestone Press.

N

Mile 5.4
ight on
10th St

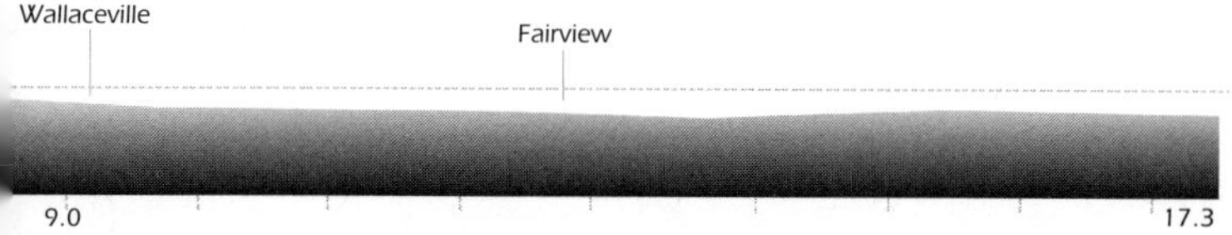

Wallaceville

Fairview

9.0

17.3

Hogjowl Road

Rating: Easy/Moderate   **28 Miles**

This ride is rated easy to moderate because there are no major hills, but there *are* quite a few short ups and downs that increase the difficulty level.

A gorgeous and idyllic ride through McLemore Cove and the Upper Chickamauga Creek Valley formed by Lookout and Pigeon Mountains. You'll see horses, Longhorn cattle, old farmhouses, churches and streams, flanked by Lookout Mountain with its exposed bluffs on one side and Pigeon Mountain on the other. The road is smooth, quiet, and relatively flat with small rollercoaster hills on the return.

Estimated Riding Times
- Beginner: 3.5 hours
- Intermediate: 2.5 hours
- Advanced: 1.75

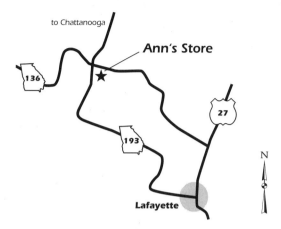

Directions to the Start
- Ride begins at Ann's Store and Service Station at junction of GA 136 and GA 193, 16 miles south of Chattanooga on GA 193.
- Be sure to park well out of the way of store clientele.

Ride Characteristics & Cautions
- There is only 1 store on the route at mile 20.
- Watch for gravel in some of the downhill turns on Hogjowl Road
- Be wary of traffic on GA 193

Points of Interest
- Very scenic valley
- Mountain Cove Farm—just past turn onto Hogjowl Road
- Friendly people

Hogjowl Road

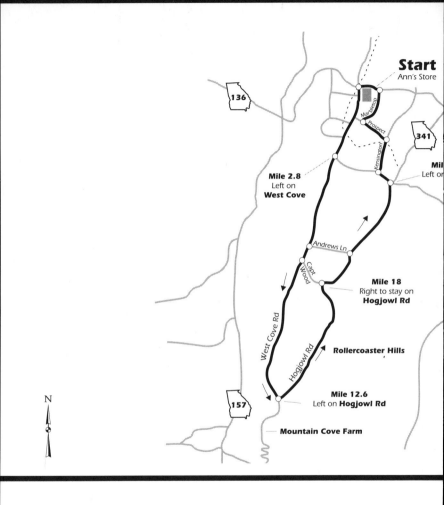

Start
Ann's Store

136

341

Mil
Left on

Marketop

Prospect

Kensington

Mile 2.8
Left on
West Cove

Andrews Ln

Capt.
Wood

Mile 18
Right to stay on
Hogjowl Rd

West Cove Rd

Hogjowl Rd

Rollercoaster Hills

N

157

Mile 12.6
Left on **Hogjowl Rd**

Mountain Cove Farm

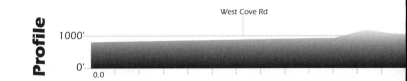

Profile

West Cove Rd

1000'

0'

0.0

For detailed turn-by-turn
directions see page 116.

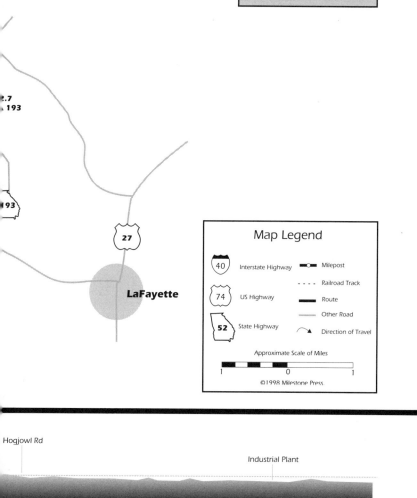

.7
193

93

(27)

LaFayette

Map Legend

(40) Interstate Highway	Milepost
	Railroad Track
(74) US Highway	Route
	Other Road
(52) State Highway	Direction of Travel

Approximate Scale of Miles

1 ____ 0 ____ 1

©1998 Milestone Press.

Hogjowl Rd

Industrial Plant

14.0   28.3

35

Blackberry Mountain

Rating: Easy/Moderate   16 Miles

This ride is rated easy to moderate. Easy because of the short length and short hills; moderate due to the fast traffic on GA 52.

 lmost every ride you can take out of Ellijay is bound to take you through an apple orchard or two. This one is no exception, as you'll pass through several orchards early on. Blackberry Mountain is the name of a private subdivision alongside the Cartecay River. You'll ride by the back side of it; look for the rather modern-looking log cabins. As you might expect, you can find blackberries here as well. Watch along the roadsides in early to mid-July for an ample supply.

Estimated Riding Times
- Beginner: 2 - 3 hours
- Intermediate: 1.5 - 2 hours
- Advanced: 1 hour

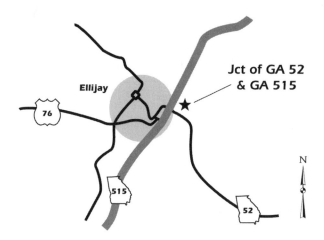

Ellijay

76

Jct of GA 52
& GA 515

★

515

52

N

Directions to the Start
- Ride begins at jct. of GA 52 and GA 515. You may want to park somewhere in town and just start your odometer here.

Ride Characteristics & Cautions
- GA 52 can have some pretty fast traffic, especially when people are going to and from work in the early morning and late afternoon. It also has little or no shoulder.
- Blackberry Mountain Road is bumpy
- There are few stores along this route until you get to Ellijay

Points of Interest
- Apple Orchards
- Rolling farmland and mountain views
- Cartecay River crossing

Blackberry Mountain

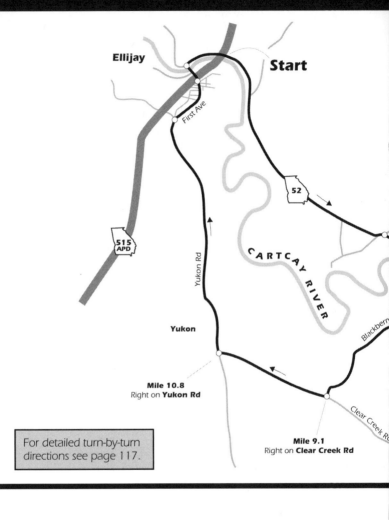

Ellijay

Start

First Ave

52

515
APD

Yukon Rd

CARTCAY RIVER

Blackberr

Yukon

Mile 10.8
Right on **Yukon Rd**

Clear Creek Rd

Mile 9.1
Right on **Clear Creek Rd**

For detailed turn-by-turn
directions see page 117.

Profile

Cartecay River

Clear Creek Rd

1000'

0.0

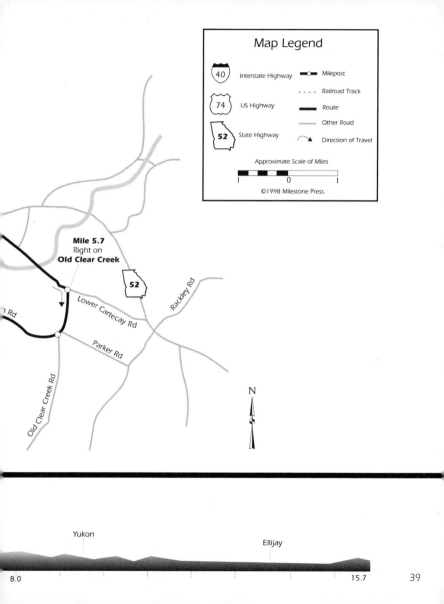

Map Legend

40 Interstate Highway
74 US Highway
52 State Highway

Milepost
Railroad Track
Route
Other Road
Direction of Travel

Approximate Scale of Miles

©1998 Milestone Press.

Mile 5.7
Right on
Old Clear Creek

52

Rackley Rd

Lower Cartecay Rd

n Rd

Parker Rd

Old Clear Creek Rd

N

Yukon

Ellijay

8.0

15.7

Porter Springs

Rating: Easy/Moderate   24 Miles

This ride is rated easy to moderate due to its length, some hills and some highway riding.

The only shadows you'll see on this route are those of the Blue Ridge Mountains. (*Read: this ride can be very hot in the summer.*) From many points along the roadway you can see the wall of mountains looming in the distance. You'll ride to their very foot before turning back along Porter Springs Road. Many years ago, Porter Springs was famous among the Indians as a fountain of youth. And if you're looking for a really big patch of famous Georgia kudzu, you'll find it on this ride along with plenty of cow pastures, open woods, grassland and views.

Estimated Riding Times
- Beginner: 3.5 - 4 hours
- Intermediate: 2.5 hours
- Advanced: 1.75 hours

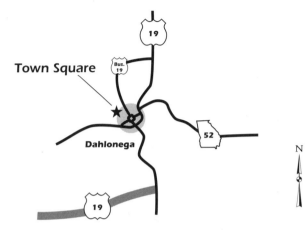

Directions to the Start
- Ride begins at the town square in Dahlonega
- Most of the parking around the square has a 3-hour limit, so look on the back streets for longer term free parking

Ride Characteristics & Cautions
- Bring plenty of provisions. There are no stores along the route
- If it's hot and sunny, be prepared with drinking water and sunscreen. There's no shade.
- GA 52 has a wide shoulder and also the potential for fast traffic

Points of Interest
- Dahlonega, site of America's first gold rush
- Rock House Antiques on Rock House Road
- The many shops in and around Dahlonega

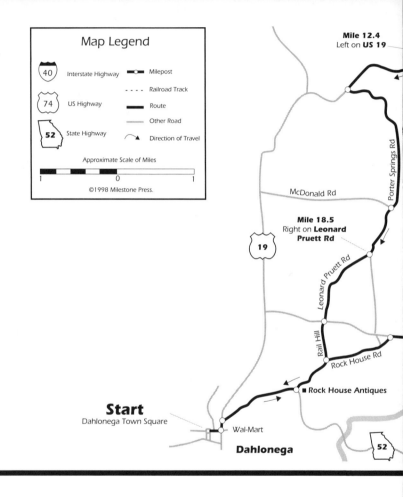

Map Legend

$\boxed{40}$ Interstate Highway   ▬●▬ Milepost

$\boxed{74}$ US Highway   - - - - Railroad Track

$\boxed{52}$ State Highway   ▬▬ Route

       ▬▬ Other Road

       ⤵ Direction of Travel

Approximate Scale of Miles

1   0   1

©1998 Milestone Press.

Mile 12.4
Left on **US 19**

McDonald Rd

Porter Springs Rd

$\boxed{19}$

Mile 18.5
Right on **Leonard Pruett Rd**

Leonard Pruett Rd

Rail Hill

Rock House Rd

■ Rock House Antiques

Start
Dahlonega Town Square

Wal-Mart

Dahlonega

$\boxed{52}$

Profile

2000'

Rock House

Chestatee River

1000'   0.0

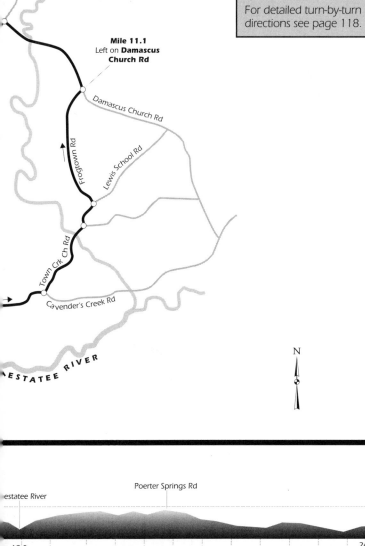

For detailed turn-by-turn directions see page 118.

Mile 11.1
Left on **Damascus
Church Rd**

Damascus Church Rd

Lewis School Rd

Frogtown Rd

Town Crk Ch Rd

Cavender's Creek Rd

ESTATEE RIVER

N

estatee River

Poerter Springs Rd

12.0

24.0

Sautee Nacoochee

Rating: Easy/Moderate   18 Miles

This ride is rated easy to moderate due to its short length, a few hills and the potential for tourist traffic near Helen.

On this route, you'll ride the rolling countryside around Georgia's "alpine" town of Helen. This unique village is a town completely transformed into a tourist attraction. All the buildings are constructed to look as if they are in the Alps. It's quite amusing to ride out of town and then back into it listening to the distorted sounds of Bavarian music, which is piped right into the streets. The route passes white-steepled churches and big, old mountain farms as it works its way out into the beautiful Sautee and Nacoochee Valleys. Be sure to stop in at the Old Sautee Store and check out the two Indian mounds you'll pass on Highway 17. Neither of the mounds are open to the public, but you can see them rising up out of the pastures alongside the road. If you have the time, you might want to try tubing on the Chattahoochee River after your ride.

Estimated Riding Times
- Beginner: 2 - 3 hours
- Intermediate: 1.5 - 2 hours
- Advanced: 1 -1.5 hours

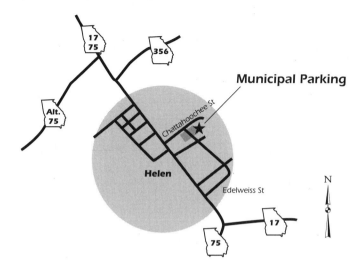

Directions to the Start
- Ride begins at the municipal parking area on Chattahoochee Street in downtown Helen

Ride Characteristics & Cautions
- Traffic on the main street in Helen can be bumper to bumper in peak tourist season. In fact, a bicycle is the fastest way to get around.
- The majority of the route is on quiet country roads
- Watch for fast cars on the short stretch of GA 17/75 on your return into town.

Points of Interest
- Town of Helen, Georgia's Alpine Village
- Unicoi State Park
- Old Sautee Store
- Nacoochee Valley Indian mounds

For detailed turn-by-turn
directions see page 119.

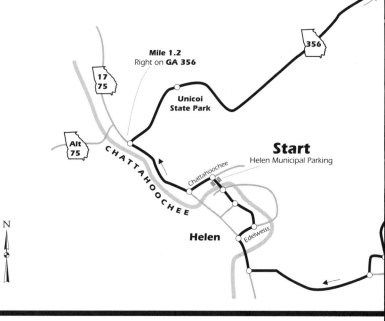

R

Mile 1.2
Right on **GA 356**

356

**17
75**

**Unicoi
State Park**

**Alt
75**

CHATTAHOOCHEE

Start
Helen Municipal Parking

Chattahoochee

N

Helen

Edelweiss

Profile

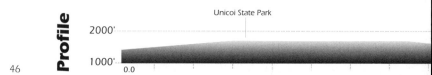

Unicoi State Park

2000'

1000'

0.0

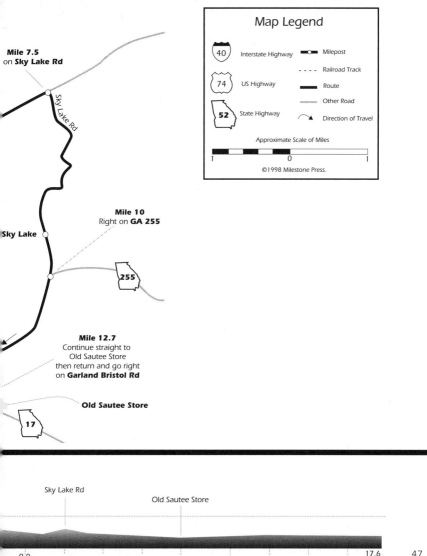

Map Legend

40 Interstate Highway
74 US Highway
52 State Highway

Milepost
Railroad Track
Route
Other Road
Direction of Travel

Approximate Scale of Miles

1 0 1

©1998 Milestone Press.

Mile 7.5
on **Sky Lake Rd**

Sky Lake Rd

Sky Lake

Mile 10
Right on **GA 255**

255

Mile 12.7
Continue straight to
Old Sautee Store
then return and go right
on **Garland Bristol Rd**

Old Sautee Store

17

Sky Lake Rd

Old Sautee Store

9.0

17.6

West Brow Lookout Mountain

Rating: Moderate   34 Miles

This ride is rated moderate due to the number of undulating "rollercoaster" hills along the brow.

 really cool ride across the top of Lookout Mountain and its west brow. Lookout Mountain is so wide and flat on top that you may forget you're on a mountain until a particularly spectacular view of the distant ridges and the valley below makes it obvious. The houses perched on the rim are fascinating examples of mountain architecture. One looks like a medieval castle—complete with turrets! At the high point of the brow, you'll pass Lookout Mountain Flight Park. Give yourself time to take a break here and watch the hang gliders soar like birds.

Estimated Riding Times
- Beginner: 5+ hours
- Intermediate: 3.5 - 4 hours
- Advanced: 2.5- 3 hours

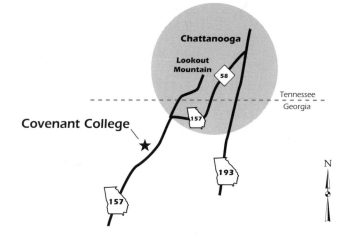

Directions to the Start
- Ride begins at Covenant College
- Park and start at Barnes Athletic Center on GA 189 atop Lookout Mountain

Ride Characteristics & Cautions
- Many people who work in Chattanooga live on Lookout Mountain. Watch for commuter traffic in the early morning and late afternoon
- Bring provisions; there are only a few stores along the route

Points of Interest
- Covenant College
- Unique architecture along the rim
- Lookout Mountain Flight Park

For detailed turn-by-turn directions see page 120.

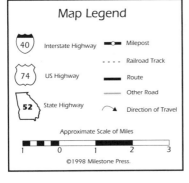

Map Legend

(40)	Interstate Highway	●▬●	Milepost
		- - - -	Railroad Track
(74)	US Highway	▬▬	Route
		▬▬	Other Road
(52)	State Highway	◢	Direction of Travel

Approximate Scale of Miles

1 0 1 2 3

©1998 Milestone Press.

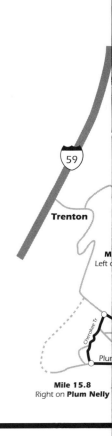

(59)

Trenton

M
Left (

Cherokee Tr

Plu

Mile 15.8
Right on **Plum Nelly**

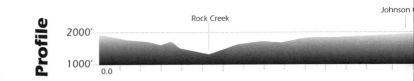

Profile

Rock Creek

Johnson C

2000'

1000' 0.0

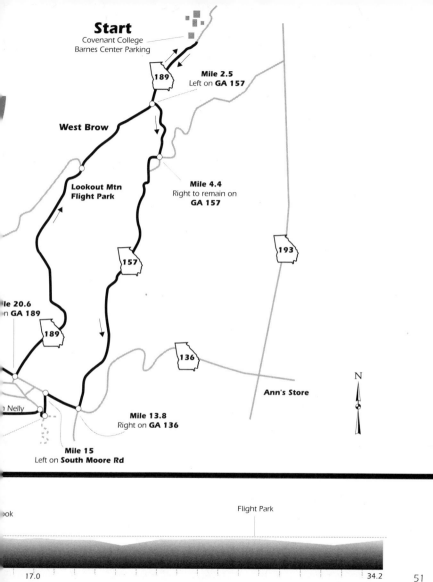

Start
Covenant College
Barnes Center Parking

189

Mile 2.5
Left on **GA 157**

West Brow

**Lookout Mtn
Flight Park**

Mile 4.4
Right to remain on
GA 157

193

157

Mile 20.6
on **GA 189**

189

136

Ann's Store

N

Nelly

Mile 13.8
Right on **GA 136**

Mile 15
Left on **South Moore Rd**

ook

Flight Park

17.0

34.2

Everett Springs

Rating: Moderate   34 Miles

This ride is rated moderate due mainly to its length and the short section of highway riding at the start and finish.

 A nice valley ride that rolls along quiet, rural roads between Johns Mountain and Horn Mountain north of Rome. You'll pass a lot of small cattle farms on roads that are alternately open and shaded, with pretty views across open fields up to the mountains above. The little community you go through on the far northern end of the ride is Everett Springs. You'll also pass through the communities of Rosedale, Floyd Springs and Armuchee. These pleasant roads lend themselves well both to hammerheads wanting a workout and cruisers out for a slow ride in the country.

Estimated Riding Times
- Beginner: 4 hours
- Intermediate: 3 hours
- Advanced: 2 hours

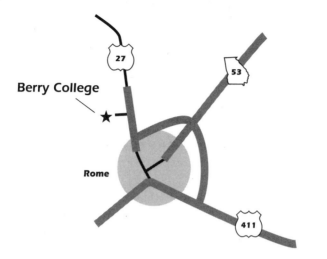

Directions to the Start
- Berry College. Park in the visitor parking lot behind either Krannert Center or Hermann Hall.
- Start the ride from the flagpole roundabout in front of Hermann Hall

Alternate Start: If you want to skip the short section along US 27, start at Mount Berry Mall, just north of the main entrance to Berry College on US 27.

Ride Characteristics & Cautions
- Majority of route is along quiet country roads
- The traffic along US 27 can be pretty bad. There is a wide shoulder to ride on, but unfortunately it is grooved which makes for a pretty bumpy ride
- There are numerous stores along the route

Points of Interest
- Berry College
- Floyd Springs Fish Hatchery

For detailed turn-by-turn
directions see page 120.

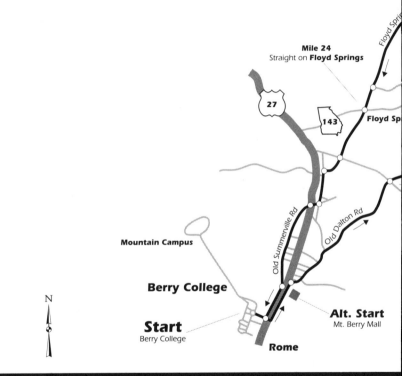

Mile 24
Straight on **Floyd Springs**

Floyd Spri

27

143

Floyd Sp

Old Summerville Rd

Old Dalton Rd

Mountain Campus

N

Berry College

Start
Berry College

Alt. Start
Mt. Berry Mall

Rome

Profile

Rosedale

1000'

0'
0.0

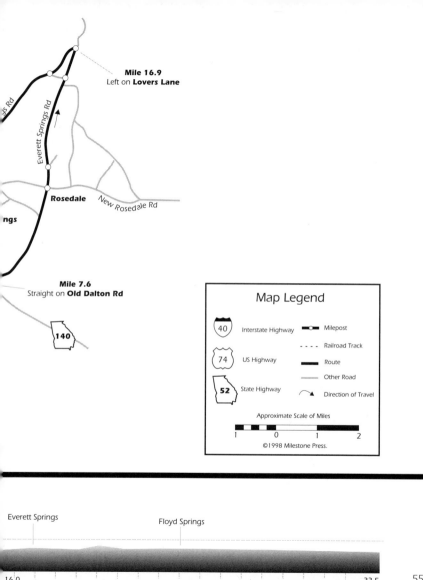

Mile 16.9
Left on **Lovers Lane**

Everett Springs Rd

Rosedale

New Rosedale Rd

ngs

Mile 7.6
Straight on **Old Dalton Rd**

140

Map Legend

40	Interstate Highway	●━━━○	Milepost
74	US Highway	- - - -	Railroad Track
52	State Highway	━━━━	Route
		〜〜〜	Other Road
		↰	Direction of Travel

Approximate Scale of Miles

1   0   1   2

©1998 Milestone Press.

Everett Springs

Floyd Springs

16.0   33.5

Texas Valley

Rating: Moderate   **40 Miles**

This ride is rated moderate mainly due to its length and a few hills of consequence.

 n the back side of Lavender Mountain, opposite Berry College, is a beautiful area known as Texas Valley. It is really two valleys, and in the middle of the two valleys are Rocky Mountain and the Rocky Mountain Lake and Recreation Area. This ride takes you first into Little Texas Valley, then circles around Rocky Mountain and on into Big Texas Valley. Both valleys are scattered with horse and cattle farms, old houses and a lot of really nice views of the surrounding mountains. It feels very remote but as the crow flies, you are only a few miles from downtown Rome.

Estimated Riding Times
- Beginner: 4 - 6 hours
- Intermediate: 3 - 4 hours
- Advanced: 2.5 hours

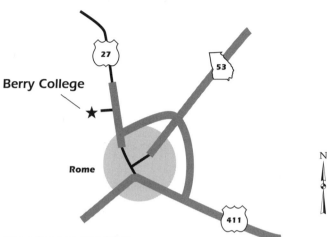

Directions to the Start

- Berry College. Park in the visitor parking lot behind either Krannert Center or Hermann Hall.
- Start the ride from the flagpole roundabout in front of Hermann Hall

Alternate Start: If you want to skip the short section along US 27, start at Mount Berry Mall, just north of the main entrance to Berry College on US 27.

Ride Characteristics & Cautions

- Bring plenty of provisions; there is only one store along the route
- Just after crossing US 27 on Little Texas Valley Road you'll cross an old wooden bridge. Take care not to drop your wheel into the grooves between the boards.
- The traffic along US 27 can be pretty bad. There is a wide shoulder to ride on, but unfortunately it is grooved, which makes for a pretty bumpy ride

Points of Interest

- Old Bridge
- Horse and Llama Farms
- Big Texas Valley Swamp

Texas Valley

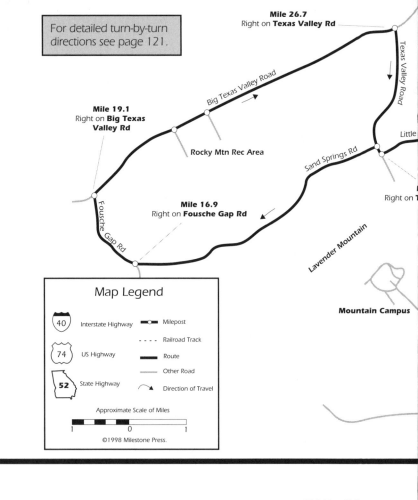

For detailed turn-by-turn directions see page 121.

Mile 26.7
Right on **Texas Valley Rd**

Texas Valley Road

Big Texas Valley Road

Mile 19.1
Right on **Big Texas Valley Rd**

Rocky Mtn Rec Area

Little

Sand Springs Rd

Right on T

Mile 16.9
Right on **Fousche Gap Rd**

Fousche Gap Rd

Lavender Mountain

Mountain Campus

Map Legend

40 Interstate Highway

74 US Highway

52 State Highway

Milepost

- - - - Railroad Track

Route

Other Road

Direction of Travel

Approximate Scale of Miles

1   0   1

©1998 Milestone Press.

Profile

1000'

0'

0.0

Armurchee Creek

Little Texas Valley

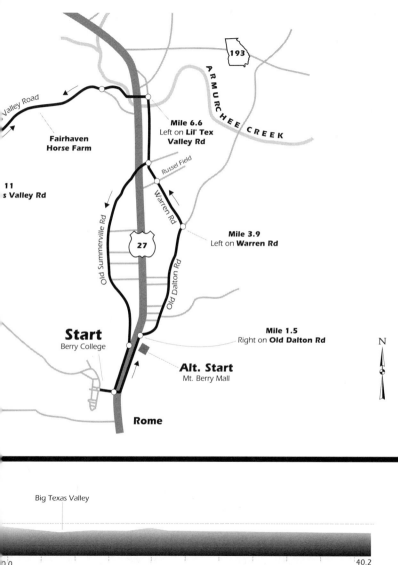

193

A R M U R C H E E   C R E E K

Valley Road

**Fairhaven
Horse Farm**

Mile 6.6
Left on **Lil' Tex
Valley Rd**

Russel Field

11
s Valley Rd

Warren Rd

Old Summerville Rd

27

Mile 3.9
Left on **Warren Rd**

Old Dalton Rd

Start
Berry College

Mile 1.5
Right on **Old Dalton Rd**

N

Alt. Start
Mt. Berry Mall

Rome

Big Texas Valley

0.0   40.2

Talking Rock

Rating: Moderate   31 Miles

This route is rated moderate mainly due to its length. You can expect some long rolling hills on Yukon Road early in the ride.

Talking Rock is a tiny village south of Ellijay consisting of an old country store, several old farm houses and a pretty, white-steepled church. This route takes you from Ellijay out through the beautiful valley known as Pleasant Valley and on into Talking Rock. The road is fairly straight but there are a number of long rolling hills. The return from Talking Rock follows the Old State Route 5. Keep moving on this road. It sees little use and there are several large stands of kudzu that are beginning to encroach on the pavement. Slow down too much and it may encroach on you.

Estimated Riding Times
- Beginner: 4 - 5 hours
- Intermediate: 3.5 hours
- Advanced: 2.5 hours

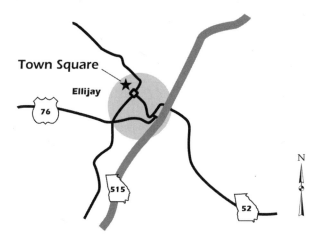

Directions to the Start
- Ride starts at the town square in the heart of Ellijay

Ride Characteristics & Cautions
- Majority of route is on minimal use state highways
- The first half of the ride is rolling hills and the last half is mostly flat
- On Old 5, the traffic tends to pick up a little as you near Ellijay on the return

Points of Interest
- Pleasant Valley—a quiet farming valley
- The village of Talking Rock—if you need a break, be sure to stop in at the old country store.
- On Old 5 there is a small lake built specifically for water skiing competition. It is oval with an island in the middle and resembles a race track. Keep an eye out for skiers as you pass by.

For detailed turn-by-turn
directions see page 122.

COOSAWATTEE RIV

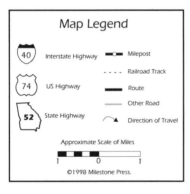

Map Legend

(40) Interstate Highway   ■–○–■ Milepost

(74) US Highway   - - - - Railroad Track

     ▬▬ Route

(52) State Highway   ▬▬ Other Road

     ⌒▲ Direction of Travel

Approximate Scale of Miles

1   0   1

©1998 Milestone Press.

Mile 17.5
Right on **Old GA 5**

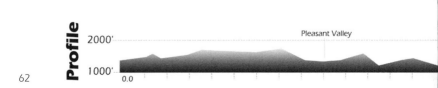

Profile

2000' ·· Pleasant Valley

1000' 0.0

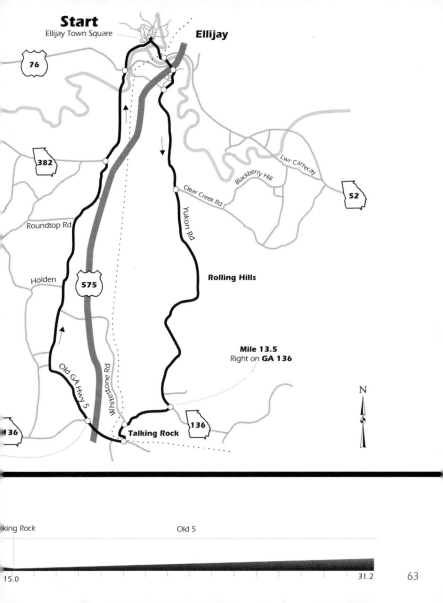

Start
Ellijay Town Square

Ellijay

76

382

52

Roundtop Rd

Clear Creek Rd

Blackberry Hill

Lwr Cartecay

Yukon Rd

575

Holden

Rolling Hills

Old GA Hwy 5

Whitestone Rd

Mile 13.5
Right on **GA 136**

136

Talking Rock

136

N

king Rock

Old 5

15.0

31.2

Upper Cartecay

Rating: Moderate   26 Miles

This ride is rated moderate due to its length and the number of steep rolling hills.

You'll ride through quite a few apple orchards on this route as you work your way up one side of the upper Cartecay River and back down the other. The valley you'll be riding through is hardly flat and feels like a rollercoaster ride as you pedal up one short hill after another. Open farmland makes for some great views of the surrounding mountains. Aside from GA 52, the roads see very little traffic and you may go for miles without seeing a car.

Estimated Riding Times
- Beginner: 4 hours
- Intermediate: 3 hours
- Advanced: 2 hours

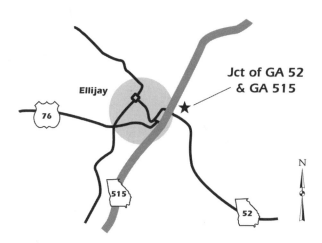

Directions to the Start
- Ride begins at jct. of GA 52 and GA 515. You may want to park somewhere in town and just start your odometer here.

Ride Characteristics & Cautions
- Majority of ride is on quiet country roads
- Be sure to bring plenty of supplies as there are few stores along the route
- **Caution:** There is no shoulder GA 52. Watch for traffic as people commute to or from work in the early morning or late afternoon.
- **Caution:** At milepost 7 on Rackley Road watch for loose gravel on the steep downhill curve.

Points of Interest.
- Apple orchards and fruit stands
- Upper Cartecay River

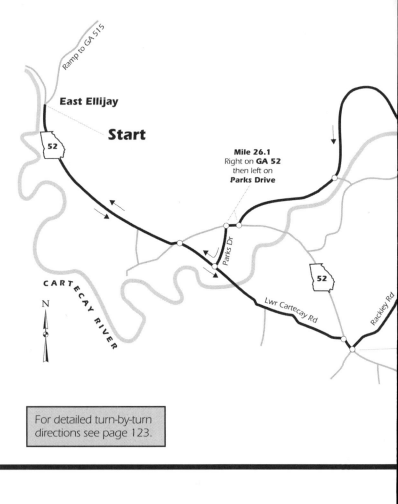

Ramp to GA 515

East Ellijay

Start

52

Mile 26.1
Right on **GA 52**
then left on
Parks Drive

Parks Dr

C A R T E C A Y   R I V E R

N

52

Lwr Cartecay Rd

Rackley Rd

For detailed turn-by-turn
directions see page 123.

Profile

2000'

Cartecay River

Rackley Rd

1000'

0.0

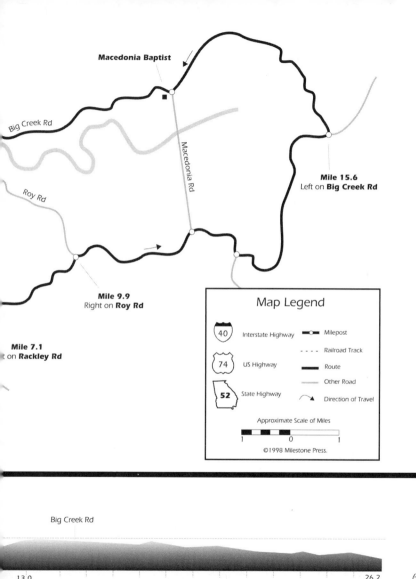

Macedonia Baptist

Big Creek Rd

Macedonia Rd

Roy Rd

Mile 15.6
Left on **Big Creek Rd**

Mile 9.9
Right on **Roy Rd**

Mile 7.1
on **Rackley Rd**

Map Legend

40 Interstate Highway

74 US Highway

52 State Highway

●—● Milepost

- - - Railroad Track

■■■ Route

Other Road

Direction of Travel

Approximate Scale of Miles

1   0   1

©1998 Milestone Press.

Big Creek Rd

13.0   26.2

Chestatee Testnatee

Rating: Moderate
17 Miles

This ride is rated moderate due to the potential for traffic on GA 52 and a number of one- to two-mile hill climbs.

 n this ride you'll always be going up or down, since there are few flat stretches. For the first seven miles you'll follow GA 52 as it dips and curves through the woods and crosses over the Chestatee River. It has a wide shoulder and a third lane on the uphills that really helps when the occasional big truck or zooming car goes by. Once on Long Branch Road, say good-bye to most of the cars and hello to more hills and the Testnatee River. On the third leg along Cavender Creek Road, things begin to open up. Look for cattle farms, sheep farms and some pretty big corn fields. Off to your right you can see the wall of mountains in the distance.

Estimated Riding Times
- Beginner: 3.5 hours
- Intermediate: 2.5 hours
- Advanced: 1.5 hours

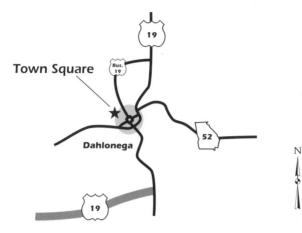

Directions to the Start
- Ride begins at the town square in Dahlonega
- Most of the parking around the square has a 3-hour limit, so look on the back streets for longer-term free parking.

Ride Characteristics & Cautions
- Be sure to watch for traffic as you are leaving and entering Dahlonega
- GA 52 has pretty good shoulders, but be careful on the downhill just past the Rock House heading down to the Chestatee River crossing and on the return after passing the Rock House heading down to Yahoola Creek.

Points of Interest
- Historic town of Dahlonega, site of America's first gold rush
- Rock House Antiques
- Beasley's Grocery, an old country store

Chestatee Testnatee

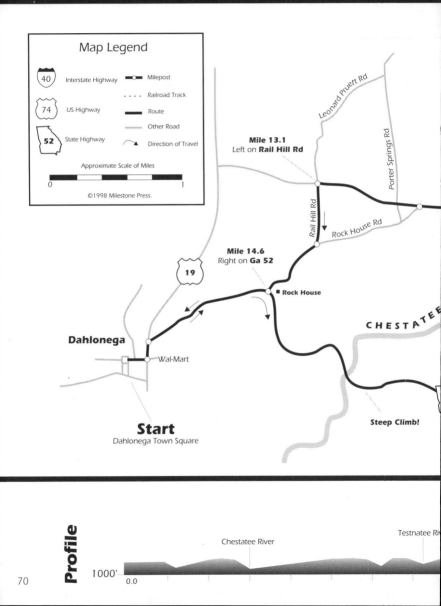

Map Legend

40 Interstate Highway
74 US Highway
52 State Highway

●─○─● Milepost
- - - - Railroad Track
━━━━ Route
░░░░ Other Road
↶ Direction of Travel

Approximate Scale of Miles
0   1

©1998 Milestone Press.

Mile 13.1
Left on **Rail Hill Rd**

Leonard Pruett Rd

Porter Springs Rd

Rail Hill Rd

Rock House Rd

Mile 14.6
Right on **Ga 52**

19

■ Rock House

Dahlonega

Wal-Mart

CHESTATEE

Steep Climb!

Start
Dahlonega Town Square

Profile

1000'
0.0

Chestatee River

Testnatee River

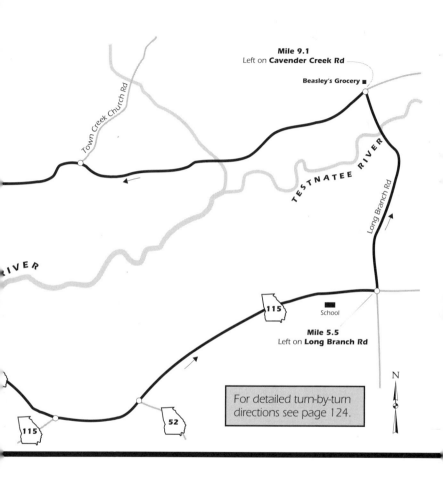

Mile 9.1
Left on **Cavender Creek Rd**

Beasley's Grocery ■

Town Creek Church Rd

T E S T N A T E E   R I V E R

Long Branch Rd

R I V E R

[115]

School

Mile 5.5
Left on **Long Branch Rd**

N

For detailed turn-by-turn directions see page 124.

[115]

[52]

Cavender Creek

16.7

Mount Yonah

Rating: Moderate   23 Miles

This ride is rated moderate due to the frequency of the hills, little shade and busy traffic near the start and finish.

Mount Yonah is a rugged, bald-faced mountain standing alone in the valley between Cleveland and Helen. Its solitary prominence makes it easy to spot. You'll circle Yonah on this ride and there are only a few places where its towering cliffs cannot be seen. Expect several sets of rather long hills and on a clear day, lots of bright (and sometimes very hot) sunshine. The farm valleys along this route are quite scenic.

Estimated Riding Times
- Beginner: 3 hours
- Intermediate: 2 - 2.5 hours
- Advanced: 1.5 hours

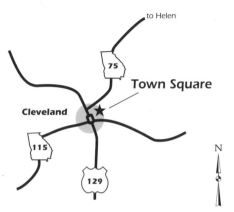

Directions to the Start
- Ride begins at the courthouse square in downtown Cleveland
- Park wherever you can find a spot

Ride Characteristics & Cautions
- Bring plenty of sun protection as the roads on this route are exposed and can get quite hot on a sunny day
- You can expect to meet some pretty fast traffic on the first mile going out of town and the last mile coming into town, as well as on the short stretch of GA 75.
- All the roads have a good shoulder except the last bit of road as you enter town on the return.

Points of Interest
- Town of Cleveland—Georgia's gateway to the mountains and home to the world-famous Cabbage Patch Dolls
- Views of Mount Yonah

Mount Yonah

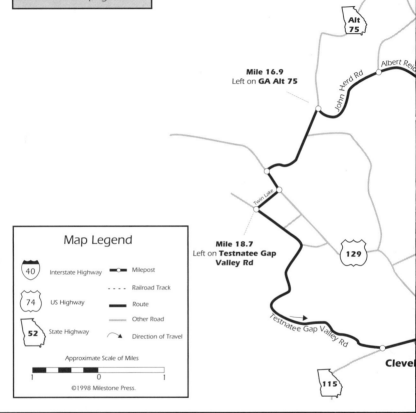

For detailed turn-by-turn directions see page 125.

Alt 75

Mile 16.9
Left on **GA Alt 75**

John Herd Rd

Albert Reid

Twin Lake

Mile 18.7
Left on **Testnatee Gap Valley Rd**

129

Testnatee Gap Valley Rd

Clevel

115

Map Legend

40 Interstate Highway

74 US Highway

52 State Highway

●━━○ Milepost

- - - - Railroad Track

━━━ Route

Other Road

Direction of Travel

Approximate Scale of Miles

©1998 Milestone Press.

Profile

GA 255

Rolling Hills on GA 384

1000'

0.0

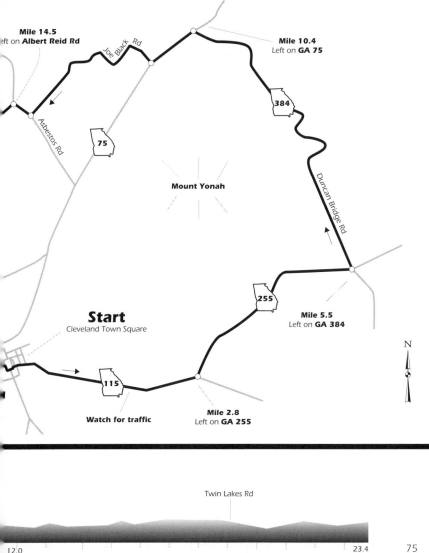

Mile 14.5
Left on **Albert Reid Rd**

Joe Black Rd

Mile 10.4
Left on GA 75

384

Asbestos Rd

75

Duncan Bridge Rd

Mount Yonah

255

Mile 5.5
Left on **GA 384**

Start
Cleveland Town Square

N

115

Watch for traffic

Mile 2.8
Left on **GA 255**

Twin Lakes Rd

12.0   23.4

Lake Burton

Rating: Moderate   21 Miles

This ride is rated moderate due to the frequency of the hills.

his ride completely encircles Georgia's Lake Burton and has many, many short ups and downs with the longest hill measuring a mile in length. Expect to use your full range of gears. You'll notice a sharp contrast between rural mountain countryside and vacation lake cottages and boat houses. In many places the ride passes right alongside the lake while in others it seems to leave the lake altogether.

Estimated Riding Times
- Beginner: 3 hours
- Intermediate: 2 - 2.5 hours
- Advanced: 1.5 hours

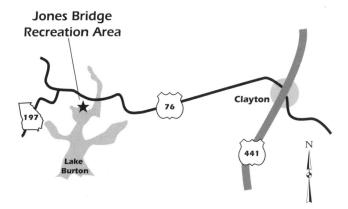

**Jones Bridge
Recreation Area**

Clayton

Lake
Burton

N

Directions to the Start
- Ride begins at Jones Bridge Public Recreation Area west of Clayton where US 76 crosses Lake Burton.

Ride Characteristics & Cautions
- **Caution:** US 76 at the start has little or no shoulder and fast traffic for the first 2 miles
- There are a number of dirt drives entering the roadway. Be sure to watch for gravel near these entrances, especially after a heavy rain.
- Except for the stretch along US 76, the route follows quiet mountain roadways

Points of Interest
- Lake Burton and Lake Burton Dam
- State Fish Hatchery along the shores of the lake
- Moccasin Creek State Park

Lake Burton

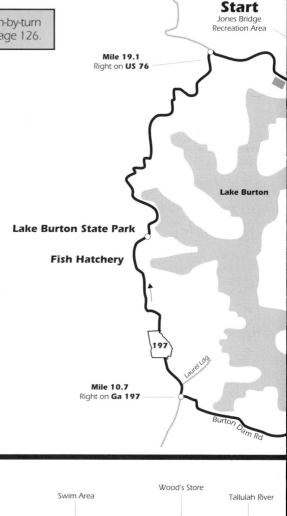

For detailed turn-by-turn directions see page 126.

Start
Jones Bridge
Recreation Area

Mile 19.1
Right on **US 76**

Lake Burton

Lake Burton State Park

Fish Hatchery

197

Laurel Ldg

Mile 10.7
Right on **Ga 197**

Burton Dam Rd

N

Profile

Swim Area

Wood's Store

Tallulah River

2000'

1000'

0.0

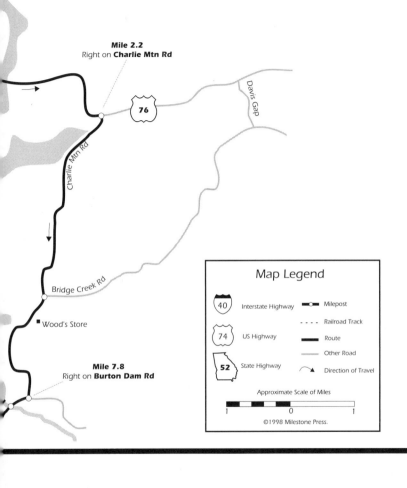

Mile 2.2
Right on **Charlie Mtn Rd**

Davis Gap

76

Charlie Mtn Rd

Bridge Creek Rd

■ Wood's Store

Mile 7.8
Right on **Burton Dam Rd**

Map Legend

40 Interstate Highway	●━━● Milepost	
	- - - - Railroad Track	
74 US Highway	━━━ Route	
	━━━ Other Road	
52 State Highway	⌒▲ Direction of Travel	

Approximate Scale of Miles

1   0   1

©1998 Milestone Press.

State Park

11.0   20.8

Germany Valley

Rating: Moderate   24 Miles

This ride is rated moderate due to several sustained climbs as well as one short but very steep climb.

 eaving Clayton, this route takes you out into one of Georgia's most remote valleys. To get there, you have to do a little climbing. You'll ride alongside small cow pastures, into dark woods and through thickets of rhododendron. Riding beside Persimmon Creek, you can feel the cool mist formed by the waterfalls and cascades. On the return you'll ride down Syrup City Road which gets its name from the number of moonshine stills that once operated in the area. Local folks called corn liquor "syrup."

Estimated Riding Times
- Beginner: 3 hours
- Intermediate: 2 - 2.5 hours
- Advanced: 1.5 hours

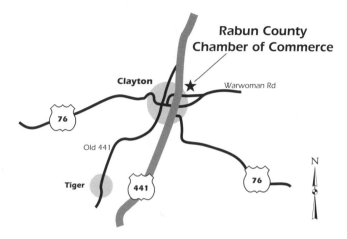

Directions to the Start
- Ride begins at Rabun County Chamber of Commerce Welcome Center on Hwy 441 in downtown Clayton
- Park in the lots farthest from the entrance to allow room for visitor parking while you are on your ride

Ride Characteristics & Cautions
- **Caution:** You'll ride two short stretches of US 76. Tourist traffic can move along pretty fast.
- There is a very steep but short climb after leaving US 76 at milepost 17.8. The descent down the other side is equally steep and is sometimes scattered with gravel
- There are very few stores along the route. Take plenty of provisions

Points of Interest
- Downtown Clayton
- Syrup City Road

Germany Valley

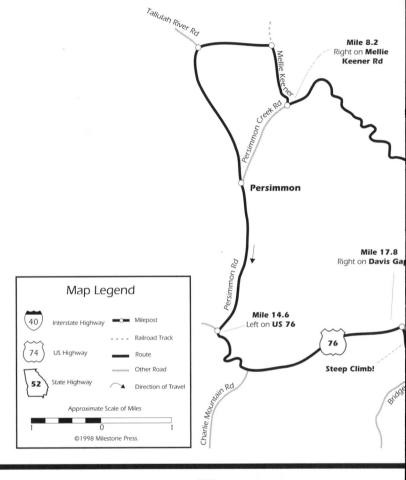

Tallulah River Rd

Mellie Keener

Mile 8.2
Right on **Mellie Keener Rd**

Persimmon Creek Rd

Persimmon

Mile 17.8
Right on **Davis Gap**

Persimmon Rd

Map Legend

40 Interstate Highway

74 US Highway

52 State Highway

⊶ Milepost

- - - - Railroad Track

━━━ Route

Other Road

Direction of Travel

Mile 14.6
Left on **US 76**

76

Steep Climb!

Charlie Mountain Rd

Bridge

Approximate Scale of Miles

1   0   1

©1998 Milestone Press.

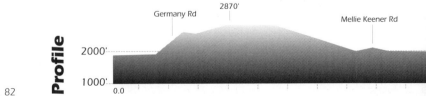

Profile

Germany Rd

2870'

Mellie Keener Rd

2000'

1000'

0.0

For detailed turn-by-turn directions see page 126.

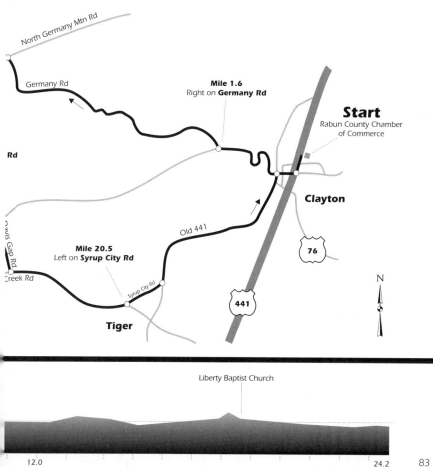

North Germany Mtn Rd

Germany Rd

Mile 1.6
Right on **Germany Rd**

Rd

Start
Rabun County Chamber
of Commerce

Clayton

Old 441

Mile 20.5
Left on **Syrup City Rd**

Davis Gap Rd

Creek Rd

Syrup City Rd

Tiger

76

441

N

Liberty Baptist Church

12.0   24.2

Rabun Lakes

Rating: Moderate

33 Miles

This ride is rated moderate due to its length along with several long climbs and many short ones.

 Half of this ride passes through rural mountain farm valleys and the other half goes alongside two of Rabun County's beautiful lakes. The valleys are sparsely populated with old country farmhouses and the terrain is fairly gentle with some long, sloping hills. Once alongside the lakes, though, everything changes. The road dips, swoops and curves like a mini rollercoaster and the vacation homes are huge and lavish. Even the boat houses are amazing to look at, giving the impression that there's some sort of competition here for the most extraordinary home. You'll return on Old Highway 441 through the little community of Tiger.

Estimated Riding Times
- Beginner: 3.5 hours
- Intermediate: 2.5 hours
- Advanced: 2 hours

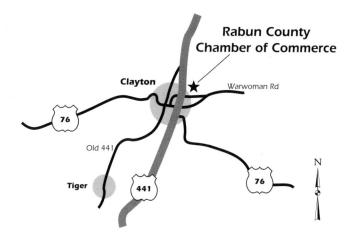

Directions to the Start
- Ride begins at Rabun County Chamber of Commerce Welcome Center on Hwy 441 in downtown Clayton
- Park in the lots farthest from the entrance to allow room for visitor parking while you are on your ride

Ride Characteristics & Cautions
- There are very few stores along this route, so take plenty of provisions
- Watch for loose, barking dogs along roadway
- The roads of this route are very smooth, making for pleasant riding

Points of Interest
- Downtown Clayton
- Horse farms and old homes
- Vacation homes and boat houses
- Lake Rabun

For detailed turn-by-turn
directions see page 127.

Mile 11
Bear left

Woods Store

Persimmon Rd

Charlie Mountain Rd

Mil
Left on **Bur**

Burton Dam Rd

Sneed
Lake

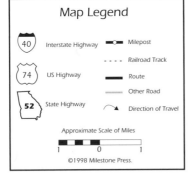

Map Legend

🛡40	Interstate Highway	●━●━	Milepost
		- - - -	Railroad Track
🛡74	US Highway	━━━━	Route
		──────	Other Road
🛡52	State Highway	◥▲	Direction of Travel

Approximate Scale of Miles

1   0   1

©1998 Milestone Press.

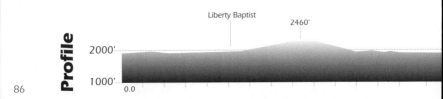

Profile

Liberty Baptist   2460'

2000'

1000'   0.0

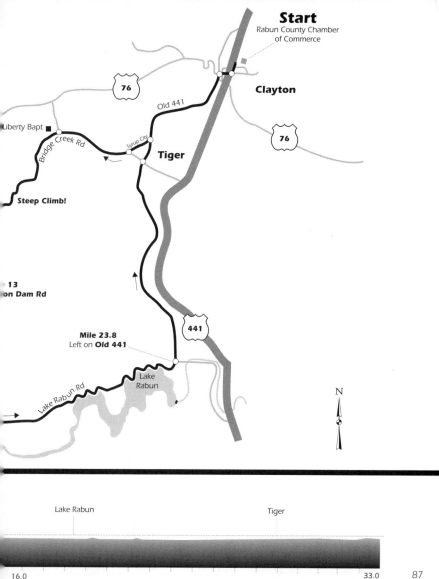

Start
Rabun County Chamber
of Commerce

Clayton

76

Old 441

Liberty Bapt

Bridge Creek Rd

Syrup City

Tiger

76

Steep Climb!

13
on Dam Rd

441

Mile 23.8
Left on **Old 441**

Lake Rabun Rd

Lake
Rabun

N

Lake Rabun

Tiger

16.0   33.0

McLemore Cove

Rating: Difficult 36 Miles

This ride is rated difficult due to the steep climb out of McLemore Cove and the number of hills along the top of Lookout Mountain.

McLemore Cove is one of the most beautiful valleys in all of North Georgia. Formed by the meeting of Pigeon and Lookout Mountains, its cool green openness is scattered with horse and cattle farms. Giant shade trees line the road as you pass classic old farm houses and well-kept barns. A steep climb takes you out of the cove and to the top of Lookout Mountain. The road then cuts back along the rim with views of the valley below. It's straight as an arrow and you can see the hills as they line up before you like waves on the ocean. The route finishes with a refreshing 4.5-mile gradual descent into the Chickamauga Valley.

Estimated Riding Times
- Beginner: 5 hours
- Intermediate: 3.5 hours
- Advanced: 2.5 hours

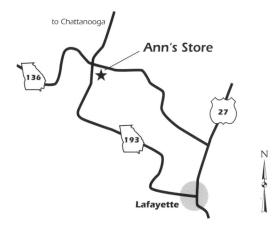

Directions to the Start
- Ann's Store and Service Station at junction of GA 136 and GA 193, 16 miles south of Chattanooga on GA 193.
- Be sure to park well out of the way of store clientele.

Ride Characteristics & Cautions
- Majority of ride is on quiet, lightly-motored roadways
- There are a number of stores spread out along the route

Points of Interest
- McLemore Cove
- Mountain Farm at head of McLemore Cove
- Overlook atop Lookout Mountain

McLemore Cove

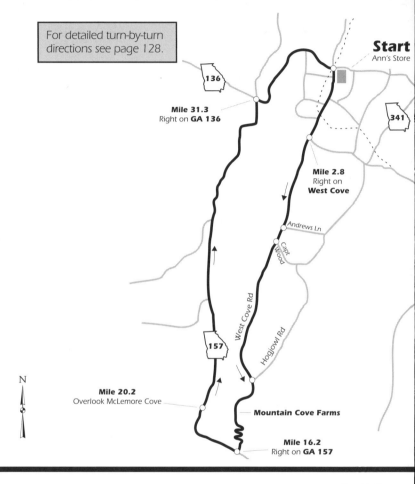

For detailed turn-by-turn directions see page 128.

Start
Ann's Store

136

341

Mile 31.3
Right on **GA 136**

Mile 2.8
Right on
West Cove

Andrews Ln

Capt Wood

West Cove Rd

Hogjowl Rd

157

Mile 20.2
Overlook McLemore Cove

Mountain Cove Farms

Mile 16.2
Right on **GA 157**

N

Profile

Mountain Farm

2000'

1000'

0'

0.0

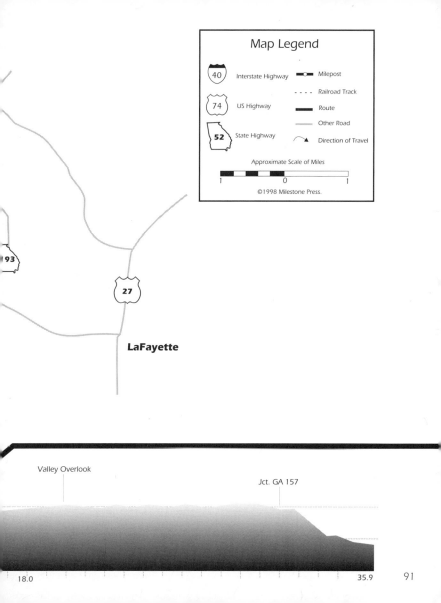

Map Legend

(40)	Interstate Highway	●━■	Milepost
(74)	US Highway	- - - -	Railroad Track
(52)	State Highway	━━	Route
			Other Road
		⌒▲	Direction of Travel

Approximate Scale of Miles

1   0   1

©1998 Milestone Press.

93

(27)

LaFayette

Valley Overlook

Jct. GA 157

18.0   35.9

Johns Mountain Loop

Rating: Difficult **62 Miles**

This ride is rated difficult due its length.

 Starting at Berry College, you'll completely encircle Johns Mountain, north of Rome, on this route. First you'll ride up the green valley of Johns Creek all the way to the little community of Villanow. The return is through the even broader Armuchee Creek valley. Expansive cattle farms, large open areas and good views of the surrounding mountains are characteristic of both these valleys. You'll see a lot of old farmhouses and at times you'll ride for long periods within spitting distance of both Johns and Armuchee Creek.

Estimated Riding Times
- Beginner: 6 hours
- Intermediate: 5 hours
- Advanced: 4 hours

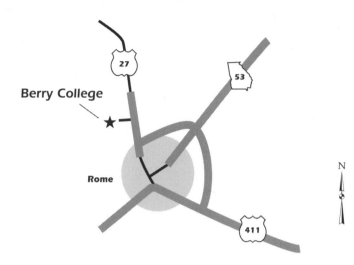

Directions to the Start
- Berry College. Park in the visitor parking lot behind either Krannert Center or Hermann Hall.
- Start the ride from the flagpole roundabout in front of Hermann Hall

Alternate Start: If you want to skip the short section along US 27, start at Mount Berry Mall, just north of the main entrance to Berry College on US 27.

Ride Characteristics & Cautions
- Majority of ride is on quiet, lightly motored roadways
- The traffic along US 27 can be pretty bad. There is a wide shoulder to ride on, but unfortunately it is grooved which makes for a pretty bumpy ride.

Points of Interest
- Berry College
- The Pocket Recreation Area and Lake Marvin
- Villanow country store

Johns Mountain Loop

For detailed turn-by-turn
directions see page 128.

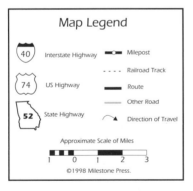

Map Legend

(40) Interstate Highway	●— Milepost
	- - - - Railroad Track
(74) US Highway	▬▬ Route
	▬▬ Other Road
(52) State Highway	⌒ Direction of Travel

Approximate Scale of Miles

1   0   1   2   3

©1998 Milestone Press.

Mile 53.5
Left on **US 27**
then left again on sr
road parallel to US

Start
Berry College

Profile

1000'

0'

0.0

Rosedale

The Pock

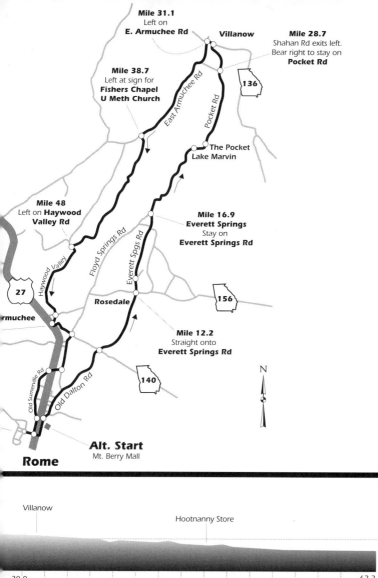

Mile 31.1
Left on
E. Armuchee Rd

Villanow

Mile 28.7
Shahan Rd exits left.
Bear right to stay on
Pocket Rd

Mile 38.7
Left at sign for
**Fishers Chapel
U Meth Church**

East Armuchee Rd

Pocket Rd

136

**The Pocket
Lake Marvin**

Mile 48
Left on **Haywood
Valley Rd**

Floyd Springs Rd

Everett Spgs Rd

**Mile 16.9
Everett Springs**
Stay on
Everett Springs Rd

Haywood Valley

27

156

rmuchee

Rosedale

Mile 12.2
Straight onto
Everett Springs Rd

140

N

Old Sumerville Rd

Old Dalton Rd

Alt. Start
Mt. Berry Mall

Rome

Villanow

Hootnanny Store

30.0

62.2

Blue Ridge Loop

Rating: Difficult   58 Miles

This ride is rated difficult due its length and the number of rolling hills.

This route will take you from Ellijay to Blue Ridge and back through very scenic, rural mountain countryside. You'll ride through one little valley after another, both going out and coming in. The hills in between will certainly get your attention. On the return from Blue Ridge the route follows alongside the Toccoa and Cartecay Rivers. These mountain streams are clear and cool and are broken up by the occasional rapids. The finish takes you through Ellijay's famous apple country where orchards abound.

Estimated Riding Times
- Beginner: 6+ hours
- Intermediate: 5 - 5.5 hours
- Advanced: 4 - 4.5 hours

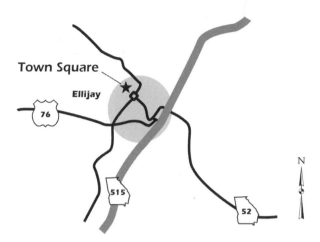

Directions to the Start
- Ride begins at town square in the heart of Ellijay

Ride Characteristics & Cautions
- The short stretch of GA 52 can have some pretty fast traffic and has no shoulder
- Majority of route is on quiet country roads
- Watch for loose gravel where dirt drives enter the roadway, especially after periods of heavy rain

Points of Interest
- Town of Ellijay
- Town of Blue Ridge
- Toccoa River rapids

Blue Ridge Loop

For detailed turn-by-turn
directions see page 130.

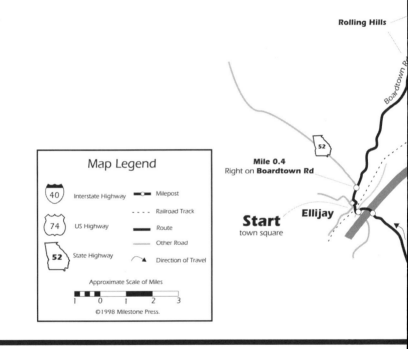

Mil
Straight on

Rolling Hills

Boardtown Rd

52

Mile 0.4
Right on **Boardtown Rd**

Map Legend

40 Interstate Highway

74 US Highway

52 State Highway

━●━ Milepost

- - - Railroad Track

━━━ Route

━━ Other Road

⌒▲ Direction of Travel

Approximate Scale of Miles

1　0　1　2　3

©1998 Milestone Press.

Start
town square

Ellijay

Profile

2000'

1000'

0.0

Boardtown Rd

Blue Ridge

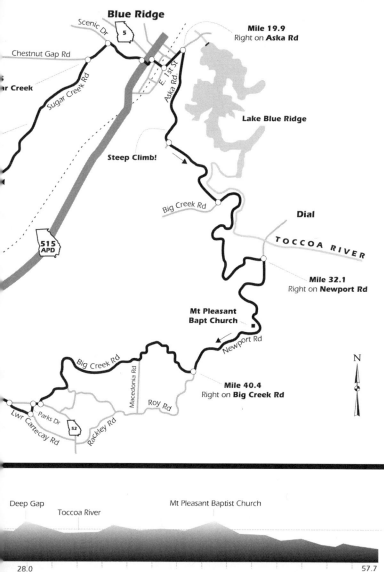

Blue Ridge

Scenic Dr

[5] (GA)

Chestnut Gap Rd

ar Creek

Sugar Creek Rd

E. 1st St.

Aska Rd.

Mile 19.9
Right on **Aska Rd**

Lake Blue Ridge

Steep Climb!

Big Creek Rd

Dial

515 APD

T O C C O A   R I V E R

Mile 32.1
Right on **Newport Rd**

Mt Pleasant Bapt Church

Newport Rd

N

Big Creek Rd

Macedonia Rd

Roy Rd

Mile 40.4
Right on **Big Creek Rd**

Lwr Cartecay Rd

Parks Dr

[52] (GA)

Rackley Rd

Deep Gap

Toccoa River

Mt Pleasant Baptist Church

28.0

57.7

Burnt Mountain

Rating: Difficult — 38 Miles

This ride is rated difficult due to the long, steep climb up Burnt Mountain and the numerous hills through Pleasant Valley.

 Starting in the midst of Ellijay's numerous apple orchards, this route progresses into a long and steep climb up and over Burnt Mountain. The views along the way are remarkable. Be sure to look over your shoulder every now and then on your way up for a spectacular panorama that includes the Cohutta Mountains far to the north. The downhill off the mountain is a blast and it leads into a real rollercoaster ride through Pleasant Valley, where you'll see quiet farms and green pastures. The route passes through East Ellijay on the way to the finish.

Estimated Riding Times
- Beginner: 5 hours
- Intermediate: 3.5 hours
- Advanced: 2.5 hours

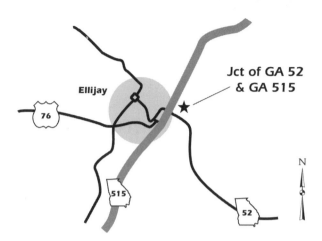

Directions to the Start

- Ride begins at jct. of GA 52 and GA 515. You may want to park somewhere in town and just start your odometer here.

Ride Characteristics & Cautions

- The short stretch of GA 52 can have some pretty fast traffic and the road has no shoulder
- Watch for loose dogs in the roadway along Burnt Mountain Road
- The road up Burnt Mountain can be bumpy in places. It is much better for going up than going down.
- Make sure your brakes are in good working order. The downhill off Burnt Mountain is smooth, long and fast

Points of Interest

- Views
- Pleasant Valley farms

Burnt Mountain

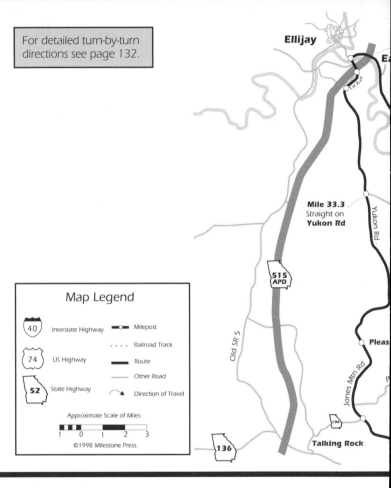

For detailed turn-by-turn directions see page 132.

Ellijay

E

Mile 33.3
Straight on
Yukon Rd

Yukon Rd.

515
APD

Old SR 5

Jones Mtn Rd

Pleas

Talking Rock

136

136

Map Legend

40 Interstate Highway

74 US Highway

52 State Highway

⊶ Milepost

- - - - Railroad Track

━━━ Route

─── Other Road

⤴ Direction of Travel

Approximate Scale of Miles

1 0 1 2 3

©1998 Milestone Press.

Burnt Mountain

Profile

2000'

1000' 0.0

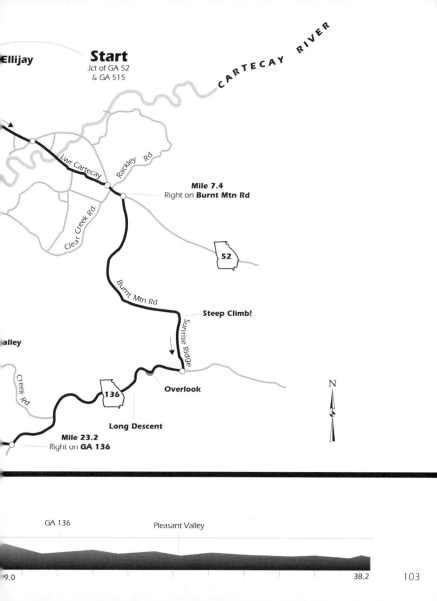

Ellijay

Start
Jct of GA 52
& GA 515

CARTECAY RIVER

Lwr Cartecay

Rackley Rd

Clear Creek Rd.

Mile 7.4
Right on **Burnt Mtn Rd**

52

Burnt Mtn Rd

Steep Climb!

Sunrise Ridge

alley

Creek Rd

136

Overlook

Long Descent

Mile 23.2
Right on **GA 136**

N

GA 136   Pleasant Valley

9.0   38.2   103

Triple Gap

Rating: Difficult

53 Miles

This ride is rated difficult due to its length and the long, steep climbs.

There's a lot to see on this ride. Starting in Dahlonega, the route heads out into rural, rolling farmland. At times you can see the blue wall of mountains in the distance. You guessed it, this is where you are going. The first of three long climbs is up to Neels Gap. It is followed by a fast descent to Vogel State Park. The next climb is through the pristine forest of Sosebee Cove to Wolfpen Gap. On the other side you'll traverse a high mountain valley and pass beautiful Lake Winfield Scott. The final climb to Woody Gap from the little community of Suches is the easiest and shortest of the three. Following it is a really long downhill, with just a few ups and downs at the end, all the way back into Dahlonega.

Estimated Riding Times
- Beginner: not recommended
- Intermediate: 5 -6 hours
- Advanced: 4 hours

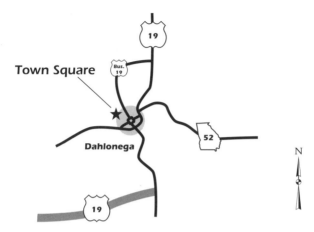

Town Square

Directions to the Start
- Ride begins at the town square in Dahlonega
- Most of the parking around the square has a 3-hour limit, so look on the back streets for longer term free parking.

Ride Characteristics & Cautions
- Route follows highways US 19 and 19/129 and GA180 and 60. Of these, US 19/129 and 19 near Dahlonega see the most traffic. GA 180 and 60 are very quiet. You'll find a nice wide shoulder on US 19/129 and not much shoulder on US 19 near Dahlonega.
- Check your brakes; the descents are quite steep from each of the gaps

Points of Interest
- Town of Dahlonega—site of America's first gold rush
- Route crosses Appalachian Trail
- Vogel State Park
- Lake Winfield Scott
- Small community of Suches
- Grave of Trahlyta, a Cherokee Indian Princess

Wolfpen Gap

Mile 25.2
Left on **GA 1**
Vogel State

Climb!

Steep Descent!

Lake
Winfield
Scott

Neels Gap

Mile 36.4
Left on **GA 60**

180

**19
129**

Long Steep C

Suches

129

Woody Gap

60

Long Steep Descent!

Damascus Church Rd

Mile 48.5
Right on
US 19 Business

19

Porter Springs

**19
B**

Cavender Creek

Start
Dahlonega Town Square

Rock House Rd

CHESTATEE

Dahlonega

Wal-Mart

52

N

Neels Gap

Vo

3000'

Porter Springs Rd

Turner's Corner

2000'

Profile

1000'

0.0

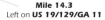

rk

nb!

For detailed turn-by-turn directions see page 132.

Mile 14.3
Left on **US 19/129/GA 11**

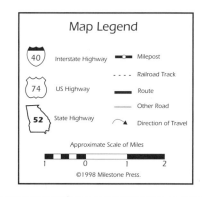

Map Legend

(40) Interstate Highway		━━●━ Milepost	
(74) US Highway		- - - - Railroad Track	
(52) State Highway		━━━━ Route	
		═══ Other Road	
		➤ Direction of Travel	

Approximate Scale of Miles

1   0   1   2

©1998 Milestone Press.

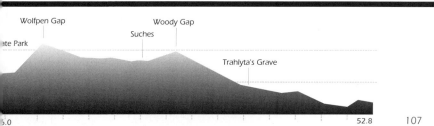

Wolfpen Gap   Woody Gap

Suches

ate Park

Trahlyta's Grave

5.0   52.8   107

Brasstown Scenic Byway

Rating: Difficult   47 Miles

This ride is rated difficult due to its length and the long, steep climbs.

This entire route follows a National Forest Scenic Byway. You'll pass alongside two wilderness areas and if you're feeling spry, you can ride to the top of Georgia's highest peak, Brasstown Bald. You'll ride beside the cascading Chattahoochee River and up and over the Tennessee Divide. And you'll cross the Appalachian National Scenic Trail twice, once at Hogpen Gap and then at Unicoi Gap. The more rugged terrain sets off the serene mountain valleys, and excellent views abound.

Estimated Riding Times
- Beginner: not recommended
- Intermediate: 5 -6 hours
- Advanced: 3.5 - 4 hours

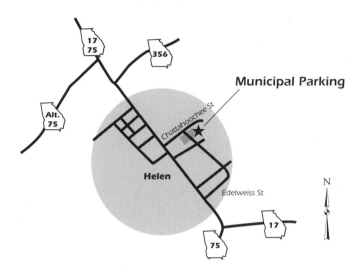

Municipal Parking

Helen

Directions to the Start
- Ride begins at the municipal parking area on Chattahoochee Street in downtown Helen

Ride Characteristics & Cautions
- There are very few stores along this route so be sure to take plenty of provisions
- Watch for tourist traffic while leaving and entering Helen
- The road up to Brasstown Bald is arguably the steepest paved road in the state of Georgia. Make sure you have a serious climbing gear if you decide to attempt the ascent.
- Check your brakes. The descents can be quite steep from the gaps and especially coming down from Brasstown Bald.

Points of Interest
- Town Helen
- Route crosses Appalachian Trail
- Brasstown Bald
- Views, views, views

Brasstown Scenic Byway

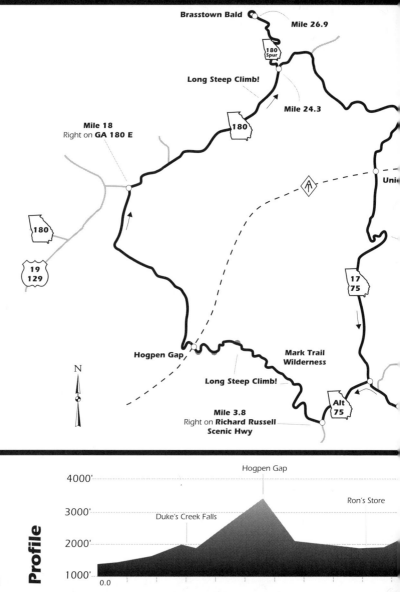

Brasstown Bald

Mile 26.9

180 Spur

Long Steep Climb!

Mile 24.3

180

Mile 18
Right on **GA 180 E**

180

19 129

Uni

17 75

Hogpen Gap

Mark Trail Wilderness

Long Steep Climb!

N

Mile 3.8
Right on **Richard Russell Scenic Hwy**

Alt 75

Profile

Hogpen Gap

4000'

Ron's Store

3000'

Duke's Creek Falls

2000'

1000'

0.0

For detailed turn-by-turn
directions see page 134.

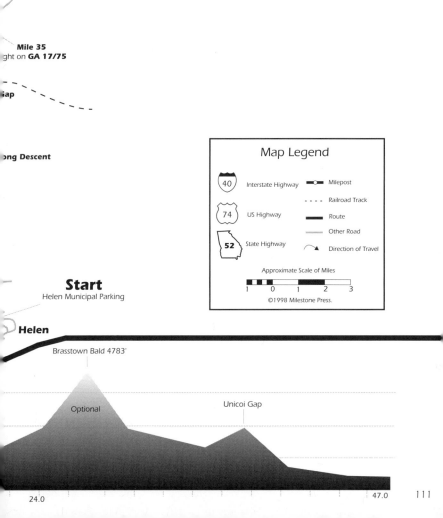

Mile 35
ght on **GA 17/75**

̀ap

̀ng Descent

Map Legend

(40) Interstate Highway   ◼━●━◼ Milepost

- - - - Railroad Track

(74) US Highway   ▬▬▬▬ Route

▭▭▭▭ Other Road

(52) State Highway   ◣━▲ Direction of Travel

Approximate Scale of Miles

1   0   1   2   3

©1998 Milestone Press.

Start
Helen Municipal Parking

Helen

Brasstown Bald 4783'

Optional

Unicoi Gap

24.0   47.0   111

Chickamauga Battlefield (pp. 12-15)

0.0	↑	Ride south on US 27. **Caution**: busy highway with no shoulder.
0.3	⊢	Turn **left** onto Alexander's Bridge Road.
0.4		**Alternate start:** when parking is available there are three spaces here.
0.7	↑	Continue **straight** as Battleline Road exits right, then left.
1.6	↑	Continue **straight** across Brotherton Road. **Alternate start:** at picnic area on the left.
2.5	↑	Continue **straight** as Jay's Mill Road enters left.
2.8	⊢	Turn **right** onto Viniard-Alexander Road. (This road is somewhat rough.)
4.8	⊤	Turn **left** onto US 27. **Caution**: busy highway with no shoulder.
5.0	⊢	Turn **right** onto Glenn-Viniard Road.
5.8	↑	Pass Wilder Brigade Monument and Tower.
6.1	↑	Continue **straight** as road enters from the left.
6.1+	↑	Continue **straight** on what is now Glenn-Kelly Road. Chickamauga-Vittletoe road exits left. Recreation field and picnic area on the right.
6.7	↑	Continue **straight** across Dyer Road.
7.4	⊢	Turn **left** to Snodgrass Cabin.
7.9	∩	Snodgrass Cabin. It's a bit of a climb to here. **Turn around**.
8.3	⊤	Back at Glenn-Kelly Road. Turn **left**. **Caution**: fast downhill; watch for cars coming up.
9.0	⊤	Turn **left** onto US 27 at the stop sign. **Caution**: busy highway with no shoulder.
9.2	⊢	Turn **left** into visitor center
9.3		Finish

Berry College (pp. 16-19)

0.0	⊙→	Ride toward Ford Buildings.
0.2	↖	Bear **left** in front of the Ford Buildings.
0.4	↖	Bear **left** on the far side of the Ford Buildings.
0.7	↖	Turn **left** toward main campus.
1.3	↦	Turn **right** toward Ladd Center and the turn onto paved bike path to the Mountain Campus.
4.4	↗	Bear **right** at Mountain Campus Windshape Center.
4.6	↗	Bear **right** toward Frost Chapel. Swan Lake is on the right.
4.9	↤	Frost Chapel is on the right. Turn **left** uphill.
5.0	↖	Bear **left.**
5.1	↗	Bear **right** at Friendship Hall.
5.4	↗	Bear **right** at bottom of downhill toward water wheel.
5.6	↤	Turn **left**, uphill through remodeled old dairy. The old water wheel is straight ahead on the dirt road.
5.7	←⊙	Winshape Conference Center. This is the old dairy.
6.0	↑	Continue **straight** past road to Possum Trot and horse stables on the right.
6.2	↦	Turn **right** out of Mountain Campus and onto paved bike path.
9.3	↦	Turn **right** after passing Ladd Center.
9.4	↦	Turn **right** at stop sign around back of chapel.
9.5	↦	Turn **right** beside dorm building.
9.6	↑	Continue **straight** around intramural fields.
10.1	←⊙	Bear **left** around Hoge Building.
10.3	↑	Continue **straight**.
10.5	↑	Continue **straight**.
10.8		Finish.

Corbin Hill (pp. 20-23)

0.0		From Courthouse Square, take Corbin Hill Road between courthouse and Chamber of Commerce.
0.2	⤷	Turn **right** on Seminary Circle.
0.3	↰	Turn **left** on Skyline Drive.
0.6	↰	Turn **left** on Logan Circle.
0.7	↑	Continue **straight** onto Old Tails Creek Road.
0.8	↑	Continue **straight** past Lucille Avenue on the left.
1.1	↑	Continue **straight** past Hancock Drive.
1.2	↑	Continue **straight** past Vista Road on the right.
1.6	⤷	Turn **right** through apple orchard.
2.3	↑	Continue **straight** past road on right.
2.4	↑	Continue **straight** past road on left.
3.7	↗	Bear **right** as road enters from the left.
3.8	✚	Continue **straight** across GA 52 near New Hope Grocery on County Road 27.
5.2	↱	Turn **right** at stop sign at the bottom of hill.
6.2	↑	Continue **straight** as road veers off to right.
7.3	↱	Turn **right** onto Boardtown Road. **Caution**: this comes up fast on a steep downhill.
8.3	↰	Turn **left** onto Dalton Road/GA 52 at stop sign.
8.6		Finish.

Old 5 Roundtop (pp. 24-27)

0.0		Ride out Old SR 5 South from Courthouse Square.
1.0	✚ ▯	Continue **straight** under traffic light across US 76/GA182.
1.3	↑	Continue **straight** past County Park and fairgrounds.
4.2	↑	Continue **straight** as GA 382 exits to the right.
5.8	↑	Continue **straight** as GA 382 exits to the left.
6.4	↑	Continue **straight** past Roundtop Road as it exits to the right.
8.9	⤷	Turn **right** onto Holden Road.

10.0	↱ 🛑	Turn **right** onto Roundtop Road at stop sign.
10.6	↑	Top of long gradual climb.
11.1	↑	Continue **straight** past Roundtop Grocery.
12.6	↰	Turn **left** onto Knight Road. (Knight Road is rough and bumpy in places.)
14.3	↑	Continue **straight**. Sunlight Road exits to the right.
15.2	↱ 🛑	Turn right at stop sign onto GA 382
17.3	↑	Continue **straight** on GA 382. Sunlight Road enters on the right.
18.1	↰ 🛑	Turn **left** onto Old GA 5 at stop sign. **Caution**: this turn is at the bottom of a fast downhill.
21.3	↑▯	Continue **straight** under traffic light and across US 76.
22.4		Finish.

Chickamauga Valley (pp. 28-31)

0.0		Ride south on US 27. **Caution**: This is a busy highway with no shoulder.
0.3	↦	Turn **right** on Glenn-Kelly Road. Ride to right in the bike lane.
0.9	↑	Road to Snodgrass Cabin exits to the right.
1.0	↑	Continue **straight** past road to cabin on the right.
1.7	↑	Continue **straight** at crossroads.
2.2	↑↦	Continue **straight** for about 200 yards past first turn for Chickamauga Vittletoe Road on the right (recreation field on the left) **then turn right** at 2nd turn onto Chickamauga Vittletoe Road.
2.7	↑	Continue **straight** past Wilder Brigade Monument and Tower on the left.
3.5	↕	Leave Battlefield Park and cross divided highway to remain on a Wilder Road.
4.6	↕▯	Continue **straight** across Five Point Road onto Crittenton Avenue at the traffic light.

Chickamauga Valley (continued)

5.4	⬏	Bear **right** around curve onto West 10th Street.
5.7	⬊	**Caution**: Cross four railroad tracks and enter downtown Chickamauga.
5.8	⬍🚦	Continue **straight** across GA 341 onto Gordon Street at traffic light.
6.2	⬍🛑	Continue **straight** across West 6th Street at 4-way stop.
6.5	⬅🛑	Turn **left** onto Wheeler Avenue at the stop sign.
6.7	⬏🛑	Turn **right** onto Grand Center Road at the stop sign. Head out of town.
8.4	⮕🛑	Turn **right** onto Marbletop Road at the 4-way stop sign.
9.4	⬅🛑	Turn **left** onto GA 341 at the stop sign.
9.8	⮕	Turn **right** onto Mission Ridge Road just after Lil' Pig Store.
12.9	⮕	Turn **right** onto Lytle Road.
14.2	⬊	**Caution**: cross railroad tracks, then pass under 4-lane.
14.6	↑	Continue **straight** as road enters from the right.
15.1	⊣	Turn **left** just before big battlefield.
15.5	⊦	Turn **left** onto Glenn-Kelly Road at the stop sign.
17.0	⬅	Turn left on US 27.
17.3		Finish.

Hogjowl Road (pp. 32-35)

0.0		Ride south on GA 193.
1.1	↑	Continue **straight** past Prospect Road which enters on the left.
1.8	⬊🛑	Continue **straight** at stop sign. **Caution**: cross railroad tracks.
2.8	⮕	Turn **right** onto West Cove Road.
4.2	↑	Continue **straight** as Akimo Road enters left.

6.3	↑	Continue **straight** as Andrews Lane enters from the left.
6.8	↑	Continue **straight** past Crow Gap Road on the right and Captain Wood Road on the left.
12.5	⊣	Turn **left** onto Hogjowl Road. To see beautiful Mountain Cove Farm, continue straight here to the farm and then return. It is not very far.
18.0	↱	Turn **right** to remain on Hogjowl Road.
20.2	↑	Continue **straight** as Andrews Lane enters from the left.
20.4	↑	Continue straight. Bluebird Road is on the right.
22.7	⬅🛑	Turn **left** onto GA 193 at the stop sign. Davis Cross Roads store is just across the road.
23.4	⊢	Turn **right** onto Kensington Road
24.7	▨	**Caution**: cross railroad tracks. You will soon pass an industrial plant on the right.
24.8	⊣	Turn **left** onto Prospect Road.
25.1	↑	Continue **straight** past Al Leet Road on the right.
26.3	⊢	Turn **right** onto Marbletop Road. **Caution**: it is in the middle of a fast descent—don't miss it.
27.7	⬅🛑	Turn **left** onto GA 136 at the stop sign.
28.3		Finish.

Blackberry Mountain (pp. 36-39)

0.0		Ride east on GA 52. There's a bike lane part of the way. **Caution**: Watch for fast traffic.
3.3	↑	Pass Mulkey Road on the right.
3.7	⊢	Just past Stegal Road turn **right** onto Lower Cartecay Road.
5.2	↑	Cross Cartecay River.
5.7	⊢	Turn **right** onto Old Clear Creek Road.
6.3	↑	Continue **straight** past Parker Road on left.
6.3+	↱	Bear **right** onto Blackberry Mountain Road at the Y-intersection.
9.1	↱🛑	Turn right onto Clear Creek Road at the stop sign.
10.8	↱▽	At Mount Vernon Baptist Church and yield sign, bear **right** onto Yukon Road.

Blackberry Mountain (continued)

14.1 ↑ East Ellijay City Limits.

14.5 ↱🛑 Bear **right** onto First Avenue at 4-way stop. (Look for Exxon, Waffle House, Burger King and McDonalds here.)

15.1 ⤒🚦 Continue **straight** across 4-lane GA APD 515 at traffic light.

15.3 ↱🚦 Turn **right** onto GA 52 at traffic light. **Caution**: Watch for fast traffic on GA 52.

15.7 Finish.

Porter Springs (pp. 40-43)

0.0 Ride out East Main Street, east, away from courthouse.

0.1 ⤒🚦 Continue **straight** onto GA 52 Business through traffic light.

0.6 ↰🚦 Turn **left** onto Hwy. 52/60/19 at traffic light just before Wal-Mart.

0.9 ↳ Turn **right** onto GA 52.

2.0 ↰ Turn **left** onto Rock House Road at Rock House Antiques and top of climb.

2.5 ↑ Continue **straight** as Rail Hill Road enters from the left.

4.0 ↑ Continue **straight** as Apple Blossom Road enters from the left.

4.2 ↱🛑 Turn **right** onto Cavender Creek Road at stop sign.

5.7 ↰ Turn **left** onto Town Creek Church Road.

7.3 ↑ Cross Chestatee River.

7.9 ↰ Turn **left** onto Frogtown Road.

9.4 ↰ Bear **left** at Y to remain on Frogtown Road. Lewis School Road goes to the right.

11.1 ↰🛑 Turn **left** on Damascus Church Road.

12.4 ↰🛑 Turn **left** onto US 19.

14.3 ↰ Turn **left** onto Porter Springs Road.

17.9 ↑ Continue **straight** as McDonald Road exits to the right.

18.5	⊬	Turn **right** onto Leonard Pruitt Road.
20.5	⇇ (STOP)	Cross Cavender Creek Road at stop sign onto Rail Hill Road.
21.6	⇱ (STOP)	Turn **right** at stop sign on Rock House Road.
22.0	⇱ (STOP)	Turn **right** at stop sign on GA 52.
23.1	⬏ (STOP)	Turn **left** at stop sign on Hwy. 19/60/52.
23.2	⊬ ⊡	Turn **right** at traffic light on GA 52 Business.
23.9	⇇ ⊡	Continue **straight** under traffic light into town.
24.0		Finish at courthouse square.

Sautee Nacoochee (pp. 44-47)

0.0		Ride up Chattahoochee Street to heart of town.
0.2	⇱ (STOP)	Turn **right** onto Main Street.
1.2	⊬	Turn **right** onto GA 356 toward Unicoi State Park.
3.0	↑	Pass through Unicoi State Park.
7.5	⊬	Turn **right** on Sky Lake Road.
10.0	↑	Pass Sky Lake on right.
10.5	⇱	Turn **right** at stop sign onto GA 255.
12.7	↑	Continue **straight** as Garland Bristol Road enters from the right. You will return to Garland Bristol Road after visiting Old Sautee Store.
13.0	⋒	Visit Old Sautee Store, then return the way you came to Garland Bristol Road.
13.0	⬏	Turn **left** onto Garland Bristol Road.
13.7	⇱ (STOP)	Turn **right** onto GA 17. **Caution**: This road can see heavy traffic and has little shoulder.
14.9	↑	Historical markers for Nacoochee Valley and Indian Trading Post, watch for indian mounds on the left
15.6	⇱ (STOP)	Turn **right** onto GA 17/75.
16.3	↑	Pass Helen city limit sign and Nora Mill.
16.4	⊬	Turn **right** on Edelweiss Street. Follow signs to Municipal Parking.
17.6		Finish

West Brow Lookout Mountain (pp. 48-51)

0.0		Ride south on GA 189.
2.5	⊣	Turn **left** onto GA 157.
4.4	⇥(STOP)	Turn **right** to remain on GA157 at stop sign.
13.8	⇥(STOP)	Turn **right** onto GA 136 at the stop sign. **Caution**: stutter bumps preceed the turn.
15.1	⊣	Turn **left** onto South Moore Road.
15.8	⊬	Turn **right** onto Plum Nelly Trail.
16.1	⅄	Bear **left** to remain on Plum Nelly Trail as Grey Road exits to the right.
18.1	⊦	Turn **right** onto Cherokee Trail.
19.9	⇥	Turn **right** onto GA 136 at the stop sign.
20.6	⊣	Turn **left** onto GA 189.
27.9	↑	Lookout Mountain Hang Gliding Flight Park.
31.7	↑	Continue **straight** as GA 157 exits right.
34.2		Finish

Everett Springs (pp. 52-55)

0.0		Ride out of campus on main entrance road.
0.4	⊢🚦	Turn **left** at traffic light onto Mount Berry Boulevard/ US 27. **Caution**: this is a busy road.
1.3	↑🚦	Continue **straight** under traffic light past Old Summerville Road on the left and the Mount Berry Mall on the right.
1.5	⊦	Turn **right** onto Old Dalton Road.
7.6	⫪(STOP)	Continue **straight** across Turkey Mountain Road/GA 140, at the stop sign.
12.2	⫪(STOP)	Community of Rosedale. Cross New Rosedale Road onto Everett Springs Road.
12.6	⅄	Bear **left** to remain on Everett Springs Road as Culpepper Road goes to the right.
15.3	↑	Continue **straight** past Everett Springs Baptist Church and Floyd Springs Road on the left.
16.9	⊣	Turn back to the **left** (reverse Y intersection) onto Lover's Lane Road.
17.7	↑	Continue **straight** as Floyd Springs Road enters from the left (route now follows Floyd Springs Road).

22.0	↑	Continue **straight** past Arrowhead Waterfowl Area on the left.
23.0	↑	Continue **straight** as Rosedale Road enters from the left. Historical marker here.
24.0	⳹(STOP)	Continue **straight** across GA143 at stop sign.
26.0	⳹(STOP)	Continue **straight** across GA140 at stop sign.
26.8	↰(STOP)	Turn **left** onto Old Summerville Road.
28.1	↱(STOP)	Turn **right** to remain on Old Summerville Road at the stop sign.
28.3	⳹(STOP)	Continue **straight** across US 27(4-lane) at the stop sign.
32.2	↱▯	Turn **right** onto US 27 at the traffic light.
33.0	↳▯	Turn **right** into Berry Campus at traffic light.
33.5		Finish.

Texas Valley (pp. 56-59)

0.0		Ride out of campus on main road.
0.4	↰▯	Turn **left** at traffic light onto Mount Berry Boulevard/ US 27.
1.3	↑▯	Continue **straight** under traffic light past Old Summerville Road on the left and the Mount Berry Mall on the right.
1.5	↳	Turn **right** onto Old Dalton Road.
2.6	↑	Continue **straight** past Glenwood School on the right.
3.9	↰	Turn **left** onto Warren Road.
5.2	⳹(STOP)	Continue **straight** at stop sign across Russell Field Road.
5.6	⳹(STOP)	Continue **straight** at 4-way stop onto Old Summerville Road.
6.6	↰	Turn **left** onto Li'l Tex Valley Road just after crossing Armuchee Creek .
6.7	⳹(STOP)	Continue **straight** at stop sign across US 27 onto Little Texas Valley Road.
7.1	↑	**Caution**: wooden bridge can be slippery.
7.6	↑(STOP)	Continue **straight** at stop sign onto Little Texas Valley Road.
11.0	↱(STOP)	Turn **right** onto Texas Valley Road at stop sign.

Texas Valley (continued)

11.3	↰	Turn **left** onto Sand Springs Road (sign for Berry College WMA here).
16.9	↱	Turn **right** onto Fousche Gap Road.
19.1	↱ (STOP)	Turn **right** onto Big Texas Valley Road at the stop sign.
19.6	↑	Swamp on the right. Look for wildlife.
19.8	↑	Continue **straight** past the entrance to Rocky Mountain Hydroelectric Plant and Recreation Area.
22.0	↑	Continue **straight** past the main entrance to Rocky Mountain Recreation Area .
22.7	↦	Turn right onto Texas Valley Road.
29.1	↑	Continue **straight** as Sand Springs Road exits right.
29.4	↰	Turn **left** onto Little Texas Valley Road.
32.8	↰	Bear **left** at Y-intersection to remain on Little Texas Valley Road.
33.3	↑	**Caution**: Wooden bridge.
33.7	↟ (STOP)	Continue **straight** across US 27 at stop sign.
33.8	↦ (STOP)	Turn **right** onto Old Summerville Road at the stop sign.
34.8	↦ (STOP)	Turn **right** to remain on Old Summerville Road at the 4-way stop.
35.0	↟ (STOP)	Continue **straight** across US 27 at stop sign to remain on Old Summerville Road.
39.0	↱ 🚦	Turn **right** onto US 27 at the traffic light.
39.8	↦ 🚦	Turn **right** into Berry Campus at traffic light.
40.2		Finish.

Talking Rock (pp.. 60-63)

0.0		Leave town square on GA 52 heading east.
0.6	▨	**Caution**: cross railroad tracks.
0.9	↦ 🚦	Turn **right** toward Hardee's at traffic light.
1.0	↟ 🚦	Go **straight** across GA APD 515 and onto First Avenue.
1.7	↰ (STOP)	Bear **left** onto Yukon Road at the 4-way stop (Waffle House is on the right and Wal-Mart is ahead on the right).

5.4	↑	Continue straight past Mount Vernon Baptist Church.
10.4	↑	Pickens County line. Road becomes Jones Mountain Road.
13.5	�	Turn **right** onto GA 136.
15.5	⟵(STOP)	Turn left onto GA 136/Whitestone Road at stop sign. (Talking Rock Baptist Church on the right)
16.1	↑	Enter Talking Rock.
16.1+	⟼⟍	Bear **right. Caution**: cross railroad tracks.
16.2	⟼(STOP)	Turn **right** at stop sign to remain on GA 136.
17.2	↑	Continue **straight** under 4-lane GA APD 515.
17.5	⟼	Bear right onto Old State Route 5.
20.9	↑	White Stone community. (BP Station, special ski lake with jumps and slalom course)
22.3	↑	Continue **straight** past Holden Road on the left.
23.4		Continue **straight** as road becomes GA 382. The 4-lane is very close through here.
26.9	↑	Continue **straight** as GA 382 exits left.
30.1	⚑▯	Continue **straight** through traffic light and across US 76 and GA 282.
31.2		Finish at town square.

Upper Cartecay (pp. 64-67)

0.0		Head east on GA 52.
3.3	↑	Turn **right** onto Mulkey Road
3.7	⟼	Turn **right** on Lower Cartecay Road immediately past Stegal Mill Road.
4.6	↑	Continue **straight** as Parks Drive enters from left.
5.2	↑	Cross Cartecay River.
6.1	↑	Continue **straight** past Aaron Road on left.
6.9	⟼(STOP)	Turn right onto GA 52 at stop sign.
7.1	⟵	Turn **left** onto Rackley Road at Crossroads Grocery.
7.6	↑	Continue **straight** past road to the left.
9.9	⟼(STOP)	Turn **right** onto Roy Road at the stop sign. (Long Road is straight ahead)
10.2	↑	Continue **straight** past Macedonia Road on the left.

Upper Cartecay (continued)

10.6	↰	Bear **left** to remain on Roy Road at the Y-intersection.
13.7	↑	Road to New Hope Baptist Church exits left.
15.6	◀(STOP)	Turn back to the **left** at the stop sign onto Big Creek Road (inverted Y-intersection).
18.9	↑	Continue **straight** past New Liberty Baptist Church and incoming road on the left.
19.5	↑	Continue **straight** past Macedonia Baptist Church and Macedonia Road.
21.3	↑	Continue **straight** past River Hill Road on the left.
24.3	↑	Continue **straight** as road enters left.
26.1	↱(STOP)	Turn **right** onto GA 52 at stop sign.
26.2	◀	Turn **left** onto Parks Drive.
27.0	↱(STOP)	Turn **right** onto Lower Cartecay Road.
27.9	↰(STOP)	Turn **left** onto GA 52 at stop sign.
28.9	↦	Finish.

Chestatee Testnatee (pp. 68-71)

0.0		Ride out East Main Street, away from court-house square, on GA 52B.
0.1	⇅🚦	Continue **straight** onto GA 52B through traffic light
0.6	◀🚦	Turn left onto Hwy. 52/60/19 at traffic light—just before Wal-Mart.
0.9	↦	Turn **right** onto GA 52.
2.0	↑	Top of hill, Rock House Antiques Store on left.
3.0	↑	Cross Chestatee River.
5.4	↑	Long Branch Elementary School on right.
5.5	◀	Turn **left** onto Long Branch Road at crossroads. (Our Place BBQ and BP Station on the right)
7.8	↑	Cross Testnatee River.
9.1	↰(STOP)	Turn **left** onto Cavender Road at stop sign and Beasley's Grocery.
10.2	↑	Continue **straight** as Town Creek Church Road enters from right.
11.7	↑	Continue **straight** as Rock House Road enters

		from left.
11.9	↑	Continue **straight** as Porter Springs Road enters from right.
13.1	◂┥	Turn **left** onto Rail Hill Road. Leonard Pruett Road is on the right.
14.2	⤷(STOP)	Turn **right** onto Rock House Road at stop sign.
14.6	⤷(STOP)	Turn **right** onto Hwy 52 at Rock House Antiques and stop sign.
15.8	⤶(STOP)	Turn **left** onto Hwy. 19/9/60 at the stop sign.
16.0	┝▣	Turn **right** onto GA 52 at traffic light.
16.6	⤉▣	Continue **straight** through traffic light.
16.7		Finish.

Mount Yonah (pp. 72-75)

0.0		Head east on GA 115 from town square.
0.4	↑	Continue **straight** past Truett-McConnell College on the left.
0.8	↑	Ride **straight** through caution light.
2.8	◂┥	Turn **left** onto GA 255.
5.5	⤶(STOP)	Turn **left** at 4-way stop onto GA 384/Duncan Bridge Road.
10.4	⤶(STOP)	Turn **left** at stop sign onto GA 75.
11.3	┝	Turn **right** onto Joe Black Road.
13.4	⤷(STOP)	Turn **right** at stop sign onto Asbestos Road.
14.5	◂┥	Turn **left** onto Albert Reid Road/ CR 84
16.4	⤷(STOP)	Turn **right** at stop sign onto John Herd Road.
16.9	⤶(STOP)	Turn **left** onto GA Alt. 75 at stop sign.
18.3	⤶(STOP)	Turn **left** at stop sign onto US 129.
18.4	┝	Turn **right** onto Twin Lakes Road.
18.7	⤶(STOP)	Turn **left** at stop sign onto Testnatee Gap Valley Road.
22.2	⤶(STOP)	Turn **left** onto GA 115
23.4	↑▣	Continue **straight** under traffic light to finish.

Lake Burton (pp. 76-79)

0.0		Ride east across bridge on US 76.
1.3	↑	Persimmon Road enters from left at top of hill, continue **straight**.
2.2	↳	Turn **right** on Charlie Mtn Road at Mark's Marina.
3.1	↑	Public Recreation area with swimming beach on right, continue **straight**.
3.2	↑	Overlook of Lake Burton.
5.8	↱ 🛑	Turn **right** onto Bridge Creek Road at stop sign.
7.8	↱ 🛑	Turn **right** on Burton Dam Road at stop sign.
8.4	↑	Cross Tallulah River. Lake Burton Dam is upstream on the right.
10.7	↱ 🛑	Turn **right** onto GA 197 at stop sign. Brooks Lil General Store is on the right.
10.9	↰	Bear **left** to remain on GA 197 as Laurel Lodge Road goes right.
15.4	↑	Lake Burton Fish Hatchery and interpretive center and Moccasin Creek State Park.
19.1	↱ 🛑	Turn **right** onto US 76 at stop sign.
20.8		Finish.

Germany Valley (pp. 80-83)

0.0		Ride south on US 441.
0.2	╀ 🚦	At traffic light turn **right** onto US 76.
0.3	✛	Continue **straight** through caution light.
0.4	✛ 🚦	Continue **straight** through traffic light to remain on US 76.
1.6	↳	Turn **right** on Germany Road.
5.0	↑	North Germany Mountain Road enters from right. Continue **straight** as road becomes Persimmon Creek Road.
8.2	↳	Turn **right** on Mellie Keener Road across small bridge over Persimmon Creek.
9.4	↰ 🛑	Turn **left** on Persimmon Road at stop sign.
10.4	↑	Tallulah River Road enters from the right, continue **straight**.
12.4	↑	Community of Persimmon.

14.6	↰ (STOP)	Turn **left** onto US 76 at stop sign.
17.8	↦	Turn **right** on Davis Gap Road.
18.7	↰ (STOP)	**Caution**: steep downhill. Turn **left** on Bridge Creek Road. Liberty Baptist Church is on right.
20.5	⤟	Turn **left** onto Syrup City Road just after Tiger City Limit sign.
21.0	↰ (STOP)	Turn **left** onto Old Hwy 441 at stop sign.
23.7	↦ 🚦	Turn **right** onto US 76 at traffic light.
23.8	⇞	Continue **straight** through caution light.
23.9	↰ 🚦	Turn **left** onto US 441 at traffic light.
24.2		Finish.

Rabun Lakes (pp. 84-87)

0.0		Ride south on US 441.
0.2	↦ 🚦	At traffic light turn **right** onto US 76.
0.3	⇞	Continue **straight** through caution light.
0.4	↰ 🚦	Turn **left** onto South Main Street at traffic light, this road becomes Old Hwy 441.
3.2	↦	Turn **right** onto Syrup City Road at Tiger city limit sign.
3.7	↦ (STOP)	Turn **right** at stop sign onto Bridge Creek Road.
5.5	↑	Pass Liberty Baptist Church and Davis Gap Road on right.
11.0	⤟	Bear **left** to remain on Bridge Creek Road as Charlie Mountain Road enters right.
13.0	↰ (STOP)	Turn **left** on Burton Dam Road at stop sign.
17.4	↑	Pass dam on right.
22.1	↑	Lake Rabun Hotel on left.
23.8	⤟	Bear **left** onto Old Hwy 441.
28.7	↑	Enter Tiger.
29.3	↑	Continue **straight** on Old Hwy 441/Main Street through intersection.
29.8	↑	Syrup City Road enters from the left.
32.6	↦ 🚦	Turn **right** onto US 76 at traffic light.
32.6+	⇞	Continue **straight** through caution light.
32.8	↰ 🚦	Turn **left** onto US 441 at traffic light.
33.0		Finish.

McLemore Cove (pp. 88-91)

0.0		Ride south on GA 193.
1.8	(STOP) ▨	Continue **straight** at stop sign. **Caution**: cross railroad tracks.
2.8	↦	Turn **right** onto West Cove Road.
4.2	↑	Continue **straight** as Akimo Road enters left.
6.2	↑	Continue **straight** as Andrews Lane enters from the left.
6.8	↑	Continue **straight** past Crow Gap Road on the right and Captain Wood Road on the left.
12.5	↑	Continue **straight** as Hogjowl Road enters from the left.
13.0	↑	Pass through Mountain Cove Farms.
15.9	↑	Road is now called Dougherty Gap Road.
16.2	↦(STOP)	Turn **right** onto GA157.
16.9	↑	Family Grocery Store on the left. First store on the route.
20.2	↑	Overlook of Mountain Cove Farms and Pigeon Mountain across the valley.
31.3	↦(STOP)	Turn **right** onto GA 136 at stop sign. **Caution:** a fast downhill and stutter bumps precede the intersection.
35.8	▨(STOP)✚	**Caution**: Cross railroad tracks, then cross GA 193.
35.9		Finish.

Johns Mountain Loop (pp. 92-95)

0.0		Ride out of campus on main entrance road.
0.4	↤🚦	Turn **left** at traffic light onto Martha Berry Boulevard/ US 27.
1.3	✚🚦	Continue **straight** under traffic light past Old Summerville Road on the left and the Mount Berry Mall on the right.
1.5	↦	Turn **right** onto Old Dalton Road.
7.6	✚(STOP)	Continue **straight** across Turkey Mountain Road/GA 140 at the stop sign.
12.2	✚(STOP)	Community of Rosedale. Cross New Rosedale Road onto Everett Springs Road.

12.6	⌐	Bear **left** to remain on Everett Springs Road as Culpepper Road goes right.
15.3	↑	Continue **straight** past Everett Springs Baptist Church and Floyd Springs Road on the left.
16.9	↑	Continue **straight** as Lover's Lane enters from the left.
23.2	↑	Continue **straight** past Lake Marvin Road on the right.
23.8	↑	Pass the USFS Pocket Picnic Area and campground on the right.
25.9	↑	Continue **straight** past dirt road to Keown Falls on the left.
26.9	↑	Continue **straight** past gravel road to John's Mountain Overlook on the left.
28.6	↑	Continue **straight** on what is now Pocket Road past Furnace Creek Road on the right.
28.7	↱	Bear **right** to remain on Pocket Road as Shahan Lane goes left.
30.8	↰ (STOP)	Turn **left** onto GA 136 toward Villanow at the stop sign.
31.1	↰	Turn **left** onto East Armuchee Road as GA 201 goes to the right and Hwy 136 goes straight ahead. Villanow Country Store is here.
32.2	↑	Continue **straight** as Shahan Lane enters left.
38.7	↰	Turn **left** at sign for Fishers Chapel United Methodist Church. This is just past Bethlehem Baptist Church and you should see a small grain silo on the right.
48.0	↰	Turn **left** onto Haywood Valley Road just past Hootnanny Country Store and cross East Armuchee Creek on a bridge.
53.0	↟ (STOP)	Continue **straight** on Haywood Valley Road at stop sign across GA 156.
53.5	↰ (STOP)	Turn **left** onto US 27 (4-lane) at stop sign. Don't leave the center turning lane as you will cross the creek and make an immediate turn back off the 4-lane.
53.6	↰	Turn **left** off 4-lane onto the little road paralleling the 4-lane.
54.0	↰ (STOP)	Turn **left** onto Turkey Mountain Road/GA 140.
54.8	↳	Turn **right** onto Floyd Springs Road.

Johns Mountain Loop (continued)

55.6	⊣	Turn **left** onto Old Summerville Road as Depot Street continues straight.
56.9	⊦(STOP)	Turn **right** at stop sign to remain on Old Summerville Road.
57.0	⊉(STOP)	Continue **straight** across US 27 at stop sign to remain on Old Summerville Road.
60.9	⊦🚦	Turn **right** onto US 27 at traffic light.
61.8	⊦🚦	Turn **right** into Berry Campus at traffic light.
62.2		Finish.

Blue Ridge Loop (pp. 96-99)

0.0	⌀⊦🚦	Bear **right** around town square and follow signs for GA 52 at traffic light. This is also Dalton Road.
0.4	⊦	Bear **right** onto Boardtown Road at Y-intersection.
2.8	↑	Continue **straight** as Flatbranch Road enters from the left.
5.3	↑	Continue **straight** past South Jones Mill Road on the left.
5.9	↑	Continue **straight** past Whitehall Golf Course, Buckhorn Estates and Salem Baptist Church on the right.
9.5	↑	Continue **straight** past White Path Road on the right.
12.2	↑	Road becomes Sugar Creek Road.
15 .0	↑	Continue **straight** past Chestnut Gap Road on the left at EV Weeks Grocery.
16.5	⊓⊦(STOP)	Turn **right** onto Scenic Drive at stop sign. **Caution**: this is at the bottom of a steep hill.
17.4	↑	Continue **straight** past Towers Road on the right.
18.4	⊣(STOP)	Turn **left** at stop sign onto 4-lane GA 515.
18.5	⊦🚦	Turn **right** at traffic light into town of Blue Ridge as GA 5/US 76 go left.
18.8	⊣	Turn **left** onto Cook Street/Mountain Street.
18.8+	▨	**Caution**: Cross railroad tracks.

18.9	✚	Continue **straight** through caution light across East Main Street.
18.9+	←▣	Turn **left** onto East First Street at traffic light.
19.7	↑⑤	Continue **straight** at 3-way stop by Pizza Hut.
19.9	↦	Turn **right** onto Aska Road at Harmony Baptist Church just before big cemetery.
24.1	↑	Deep Gap and top of climb. Pass Aska Mountain Bike Trails.
27.0	↑	Toccoa River rapids on left.
30.7	↑	Continue **straight** past road on the right.
31.1	↑	Continue **straight** past Toccoa Valley Road on the left and Walnut Lane on the right.
32.1	↱⑤	Turn **right** at stop sign onto Newport Road.
36.3	↱⑤	Turn **right** at stop sign.
40.4	↗	Bear **right** onto Big Creek Road. (Y-intersection).
43.7	↑	Continue **straight** past New Liberty Baptist Church and incoming road on the left.
44.3	↑	Continue **straight** past Macedonia Baptist Church and Macedonia Road.
46.1	↑	Continue **straight** past River Hill Road on the left.
49.1	↑	Continue **straight** as road enters left.
50.9	↱⑤	Turn **right** onto GA 52 at stop sign.
51.1	↤	Turn **left** onto Parks Drive.
51.8	↱⑤	Turn **right** onto Lower Cartecay Road.
52.7	←⑤	Turn **left** onto GA 52 at stop sign.
53.7	↦	Finish at Bike Shop.
56.4	↑	Cross under 4-lane.
56.8	↑▣	Continue **straight** at traffic light.
57.2	⟍	**Caution**: Cross railroad tracks.
57.7	↑	Finish.

Burnt Mountain (pp. 100-103)

0.0		Ride east on GA 52.
3.7	⊢	Turn **right** onto Lower Cartecay Road.
6.9	⊢ (STOP)	Turn **right** onto GA 52 at stop sign.
7.0	↑	Continue **straight** past Clear Creek Road on the right and Rackley Road left.
7.4	⊢	Turn **right** onto Burnt Mountain Road.
15.2	↑	Top of climb. Road name changes to Sunrise Ridge Road.
15.7	⊢ (STOP)	Turn **right** onto GA 136.
18.2	↑	Overlook on left.
23.2	⊢	Turn **right** to stay on GA 136 as Burnt Mountain Road continues straight.
25.2	↑	Continue **straight** onto Jones Mountain Road as GA Hwy 136 exits to the left.
29.2	↑	Pleasant Valley. Continue **straight**.
33.3	↑	Continue **straight** as Clear Creek Road exits right at Mt. Vernon Baptist Church.
37.0	⊢ (STOP)	Bear **right** onto First Avenue at 4-way stop. (Look for Exxon, Waffle House, Burger King and McDonalds here.)
37.6	⤊	Continue **straight** across 4-lane GA APD 515 at traffic light.
37.8	⊢	Turn **right** onto GA 52 at traffic light. **Caution**: Watch for fast traffic on GA 52.
38.2		Finish.

Triple Gap (pp. 104-107)

0.0		Ride east on Main Street from courthouse.
0.1	⤊	Continue **straight** onto GA 52 Business through traffic light.
0.6	⊣	Turn **left** onto Hwy. 52/60/19 at light just before Wal-Mart.
0.9	⊢	Turn **right** onto GA 52.
2.0	⊣	Turn **left** onto Rock House Road at Rock House Antiques.

2.5	↑	Continue straight as Rail Hill Road enters from the left.
4.0	↤	Turn **left** onto Apple Blossom Lane.
4.1	✚ⓈⓉⓄⓅ	Cross Cavender Creek Road onto Porter Springs Road at the Crossroad Grocery.
6.0	↑	Continue **straight** as Leonard Pruett Rd enters from the left.
6.6	↑	Continue **straight** as McDonald Road enters from the left.
10.1	↦ⓈⓉⓄⓅ	Turn **right** onto US 19/GA 60 at the stop sign.
12.0	↑	Continue **straight** as Damascus Church Road enters from the right.
14.3	↤ⓈⓉⓄⓅ	Turn **left** onto US 19/129/GA 11 at the stop sign just after crossing the river at Turner's Corner Restaurant.
18.4	↑	Desoto Falls Recreation Area on left.
22.1	↑	Neels Gap. Walasi-yi Center on right with Outfitters store.
24.8	↑	Pass entrance to Vogel State Park.
25.2	↤	Turn **left** onto GA 180/Wolfpen Gap Road.
28.2	↑	Sosebee Cove Scenic Area.
28.6	↑	Wolf Pen Gap.
31.4	↑	Lake Winfield Scott.
36.4	↤ⓈⓉⓄⓅ	Community of Suches. Turn **left** onto GA 60 at stop sign.
38.5	↑	Woody Gap.
43.8	↦ⓈⓉⓄⓅ	Bear **right** at junction with US 19/GA 9. Grave of Trahlyta, a Cherokee Indian Princess.
48.5	↦	Bear **right** onto Business 19/60 (Historic Route).
52.7	↦🚦	Turn **right** onto East Main at traffic light.
52.8		Finish at Courthouse Square.

Brasstown Scenic Byway (pp. 108-111)

0.0		Turn left out of parking area onto Chattahoochee Street.
0.2	↱ (STOP)	Turn **right** onto Main Street.
1.6	↰	Turn **left** onto GA South Alt 75 and cross the Chattahoochee River.
3.8	↦	Turn right onto Richard B Russel Scenic Hwy/GA 348 and begin climbing.
5.5	↑	Pass entrance to Dukes Creek Falls.
8.1	↑	Pass overlook on right.
10.1	↑	Pass Raven Cliffs overlook.
10.7	↑	Pass Watershed overlook on left.
11.0	↑	Hogpen Gap.
11.7	↑	Testnatee Gap.
18.0	↱ (STOP)	Turn **right** onto GA 180 East at stop sign.
19.5	↑	Pass Ron's convenience store and sign to Track Rock Gap Archalogical Area via Town Creek School Road.
24.3	↰	If you want to go to the top of Brasstown Bald, turn **left** onto 180 Spur.
26.9	⋂	Brasstown Bald Mountain gift shop and top of mountain parking lot. There is a 1/2-mile trail to observation tower. Return to GA 180 after enjoying Brasstown Bald. **Caution**: this is a very steep descent!
29.7	↰ (STOP)	Turn **left** onto GA 180.
35.0	↱ (STOP)	Turn **right** onto GA 17/75 at stop sign.
43.0	↑	Unicoi Gap.
45.3	↑	Pass Alt 75 on right.
47.0		Finish in Helen.

Milestone Press
Outdoor Adventure Guides

MOUNTAIN BIKE SERIES
OFF THE BEATEN TRACK
by Jim Parham
- Vol. I: WNC—The Smokies
- Vol. II: WNC—Pisgah
- Vol. III: North Georgia
- Vol. IV: East Tennessee
- Vol. V: Northern Virginia
- Tsali Mountain Bike Trails Map
- Bull Mountain Bike Trails Map

ROAD BIKE SERIES
- Road Bike Asheville, NC:
  Favorite Rides of the
  Blue Ridge Bicycle Club
  by The Blue Ridge Bicycle Club
- Road Bike the Smokies:
  16 Great Rides in
  North Carolina's
  Great Smoky Mountains
  by Jim Parham
- Road Bike North Georgia:
  25 Great Rides in the
  Mountains and Valleys
  of North Georgia
  by Jim Parham

PLAYBOATING SERIES
by Kelly Fischer
- A Playboater's Guide
  to the Ocoee River
- Playboating the Nantahala
  River—An Entry Level Guide

ROCKHOUNDING
by Michael Streeter
- A Rockhounding Guide
  to NC's Blue Ridge Mountains

FAMILY ADVENTURE SERIES
by Mary Ellen Hammond
  & Jim Parham
- Natural Adventures in the
  Mountains of Western NC
- Natural Adventures in the
  Mountains of North Georgia

MOTORCYCLE SERIES
by Hawk Hagebak
- Motorcycle Adventures in the
  Southern Appalachians—
  North GA, East TN, Western NC
- Motorcycle Adventures in the
  Southern Appalachians—
  Asheville NC, Blue Ridge
  Parkway, NC High Country

A NOTE TO THE READER
Can't find the Milestone Press
book you want at a bookseller,
bike shop or outfitter store near
you? Don't despair—you can
order it directly from us. Write
Milestone Press, PO Box 158,
Almond, NC 28702; call us at
828-488-6601; or shop on line at
www.milestonepress.com.

We welcome your comments
and suggestions regarding the
contents of this book. Please
write us or e-mail us at:
rbng@milestonepress.com.